UTAH

ENGLISH

UTAH

ENGLISH

DAVID ELLINGSON EDDINGTON

THE UNIVERSITY OF UTAH PRESS   Salt Lake City

The Defiance House Man colophon is a registered trademark of the University of Utah Press. It is based on a four-foot-tall Ancient Puebloan pictograph (late PIII) near Glen Canyon, Utah.

LIBRARY OF CONGRESS CATALOGING-IN-PUBLICATION DATA
Names: Eddington, David, author.
Title: Utah English / David Ellingson Eddington.
Description: Salt Lake City : University of Utah Press, [2023] | Includes
   bibliographical references and index. Identifiers: LCCN 2023003143 |
   ISBN 9781647691066 (hardback) | ISBN 9781647691097 (paperback) |
   ISBN 9781647691127 (ebook)
Subjects: LCSH: English language—Dialects—Utah. | English
   language—Utah—Slang. | Americanisms—Utah. | Utah—Languages. | BISAC:
   LANGUAGE ARTS & DISCIPLINES / Linguistics / General
Classification: LCC PE3101.U8 E34 2023 | DDC 427/.9792--dc23/eng/20230323
LC record available at https://lccn.loc.gov/2023003143

Errata and further information on this and other titles available at UofUpress.com

Printed and bound in the United State of America.

Contents

Acknowledgments

My heartfelt thanks first go to the 1,753 Utahns who took the time to reflect on their own pronunciation and usage and complete the survey that much of this book is based on. A book like this is merely an extension of the previous studies on Utah English carried out by so many others, principally David Bowie, Wendy Baker-Smemoe, Diane Lillie, and Marianna Di Paolo, many of whom gave me direction and suggestions that ultimately resulted in a better manuscript. In like manner, Joey Stanley, Dirk Elzinga, Kamil Kazmierski, and an anonymous reviewer also deserve credit for their input on this project. The book was edited by Scarlett Lindsay and the BYU Faculty Publishing Service who cleaned up the typos, questioned my prose, and ultimately made the book more readable. Most notably I thank my wife, Silvia, for being an attention widow for the few months that my mind was obsessively occupied with the ideas and concepts that I was trying to conceptualize and organize enough to finally convert into prose.

Introduction

The map in figure 0.1 represents one way of dividing the United States into various dialects.[1] Notice the variety of fun and interesting dialects in the eastern part of the country, which contrasts sharply with the apparently dull homogeneity of the West. This map suggests that once you hit the Rocky Mountains, everyone west of that point uses the same dialect. Of course, there are more nuanced ways of dividing up the country, but many have the general impression that there's not much variety in those western parts. However, nothing could be further from the truth. People from Colorado will swear they can tell a Coloradoan from a New Mexican any day, and Californians are pretty sure it's the Idaho folks who talk funny, not them.

The map represents different varieties of speech based on geography. Prior to the late twentieth century, linguists focused their attention mainly on how language varied from place to place. This focus is what we typically think of as dialectology. That began to change in 1963 when William Labov, a former industrial chemist turned linguist, published a study of the speech of the residents of Martha's Vineyard,[2] the resort island off the coast of Massachusetts where the movie *Jaws* was made. What made his study so influential wasn't that Labov was eleven years too early to meet Richard Dreyfuss and Steven Spielberg while they were filming on the island; it was what he discovered about how language varies.

He documented a case in which varying pronunciations were not found across geographical distances. Instead, he observed that people in the exact same place say things differently. As a result, Labov is known as the father of sociolinguistics, a subspecialty of linguistics that looks at how social factors such as age, social class, gender, and educational level affect the way people say things and the words and phrases they use. He showed that you don't have to travel spatially to find variation—you just have to move around in different social and demographic groups—and that the extent of the variation can be

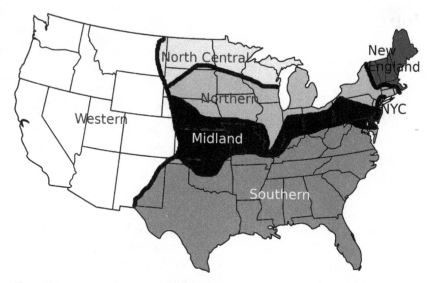

Figure 0.1. Dialect map of the contiguous United States. (Credit: Original unmodified blank map of U.S. created by Kaboom88, public domain, https://commons.wikimedia.org/w/index .php?curid=2989307. Dialect boundaries were taken from https://www.britannica.com /topic/English-language/Varieties-of-English)

staggering and quite interesting as well. In this book I consider both the social and geographical factors of Utah English.

One thing to remember about how factors relate to language is that language is seldom black and white. Take the use of *like* in sentences such as *I just felt, like, so bummed*. Many people associate *like* with the speech of teenage girls. However, if you were to sit in on a discussion between teenagers and count how many times *like* is said, you wouldn't find that the girls are responsible for 100 percent of the cases and the boys 0 percent. In the same way, if you extended your counting to include twenty-year-olds, you wouldn't observe that 100 percent of the cases came from the teens and that not one *like* came from the older group. The truth is that language varies in degrees and linguists use statistics to sort out when it looks like there is a real difference between groups.

I can easily imagine a certain number of readers throwing this book down in horror when they read the word *statistics* as memories of gut-wrenching math classes in high school, or poke-your-eyes-out boring lectures in college, dredge up less-than-pleasant emotions. Rest assured that this will not be the case. My goal in writing this book is to be scientifically rigorous by including things such as statistical analyses that linguists can appreciate. At the same time, I want to remove the academic stuffiness and make the contents accessible to the nonlinguist who is just interested in what the heck Utah English is all about. For this reason, I will include the esoteric statistics, but the reader is welcome to skip over those arcane sections to the part where the results are laid out in plain English and summarized in a simple visual graph. (BTW, I've always wanted to use *esoteric* and *arcane* in the same sentence. It would be even funner to see how many readers googled those words. BTW, *funner* is a word.)

So why a book on Utah English? The first reason is to summarize what linguists have already discovered about English in the Beehive State.[3] The second reason is that every time I read a blog post or newspaper article claiming that a certain pronunciation, or the use of a particular word, is a foolproof way to spot a Utahn, I want to bang my head against the wall. These proclamations are rarely backed up by any evidence beyond the author's own anecdotal evidence about what their cousin in Utah happens to say. So, someone, that's me, needs to present credible evidence that is worthy of being cited in a scholarly publication rather than being based on off-the-cuff speculations.

The last reason is just that more evidence of the variety found in Utah English is needed. While many respectable scholars have carried out notable studies on Utah English, too many of the studies involved the speech of only a handful of Utahns or have been carried out with speakers from only the most populated regions of the state. For this reason, more data from Utahns from every corner of the state are needed to get a sense of what is really going on there. This need for evidence was my motivation for developing and gathering data using an online survey, which I will discuss in a later chapter.

So, why Utah? Isn't Mississippi more interesting? Well, even though I lived in Mississippi, I was born in Utah. Now, my professional training was actually in the Spanish language, and I really wasn't into English, dialectology, or sociolinguistics. However, after living in five other states and moving back to Utah after fourteen-years, my linguistic ear started picking up certain pronunciations and phrases I hadn't noticed before. My new awareness meant either that things had changed since I'd moved away or that the time away from my native dialect area allowed me to return and observe Utah English with an outsider's ear. This is what got me hooked on studying Utah English.

A number of things make Utah linguistically interesting. The first is the massive numbers of immigrants who flocked to Utah in the first years of its settlement by people of American and European origin. These immigrants included lots of Scandinavians and a bucket-load of English folk. A good chunk of the settlers came from New England as well. Second, from its foundation in 1847 until the transcontinental railroad was finished in 1869, Utah was pretty isolated from the rest of the country. That isolation was not just physical but linguistic, which meant that the speech of the area could develop by itself.

Finally, the fact that so many Utahns belong to The Church of Jesus Christ of Latter-day Saints (which is a mouthful and which I will refer to as CJCLDS for brevity's sake) means that people's particular religious affiliation, or lack thereof, may play a part in how they use the features that make up Utah English. This is especially significant because practicing members of the CJCLDS belong to a community that involves a great deal of socialization, and that interaction goes way beyond a few hours spent together during Sunday worship services.

The influence of religion on the English spoken in Utah has already been studied,[4] and the influence of the CJCLDS on speech extends beyond Utah. For example, the speech characteristics of Canadian members of the CJCLDS in Southern Alberta are distinct when compared with those of others from the same area.[5] English-speaking members of the CJCLDS who live in the Mormon colonies of Northern Mexico also demonstrate some of the same vowel pronunciations that Utahns have.[6]

One question I will try to answer is whether English in Utah is truly unique. If so, what makes it different? What stereotypes about how Utahns speak are completely off base? In one study I codirected,[7] we found that there are indeed differences between the speech of Utahns and other westerners. In that experiment, a number of people from Utah and from other western states were recorded reading a passage. Parts of their recordings were played to Utahns, to people from other western states, and to people from nonwestern states. The listeners were asked to rate the speaker in each recording according to the degree of Utah accent they had.

One prominent finding was that Utahns and westerners gave the speakers from Utah higher Utah accent ratings than they did to speakers from other western states. This is solid evidence that Utah English does have distinguishing characteristics, and that people pick up on them. However, the listeners who were not westerners couldn't distinguish between Utahns and other westerners, which means that although Utah English is somewhat distinct from the English spoken in other western states, it is similar enough that people who don't have a lot of exposure to Utah English can't tell the difference.

In this book I'll examine what some of those differences are, as well as the supposed differences that really aren't. Many people mistakenly assume that everyone in Utah speaks the same way, which is why the book's central focus is to examine how English varies within the state itself.

I use the term *Utah English* for the sake of simplicity. Dialectal characteristics rarely coincide with political boundaries, and Utah is no different. In fact, many of the Utah English traits I discuss extend north into southern Idaho and east into Nevada. I recently saw an online post from a resident of Grand Junction, Colorado, complaining that people there talk like Utahns. Other traits are common only in certain parts of Utah. In fact, the theme that runs throughout the book is not one of monolithic unity of speech in the state but of social and geographic diversity. Nevertheless, all of this diversity takes place in the state, so I'll stick with the imprecise term *Utah English*.

As I mentioned earlier, I'm writing this book in a way that someone without a background in language sciences can understand and appreciate just as much as someone with a PhD in linguistics can. You've got to admit that studying dialects is fun, and I don't want to put a damper on how enjoyable linguistic research can be by framing the discussion of Utah English in dull, academic prose. This is why I've chosen a writing style that is less formal and less academic-sounding whenever possible. For example, I refer to myself as *I* and to the reader as *you*, and I avoid the illusion that books are not entities whose writers and readers meet on the pages of the text.

I'm also not opposed to using the pronoun *they* to refer to a single person whose gender I do not know, rather than resorting to the clunky phrases *he or she* and *his or her*. Moreover, if I am pressed about using *they* for this purpose, I will vehemently justify it. Singular *they* has been used for generations by literary giants of English literature such as Chaucer, Dickinson, and Shakespeare, and if you ask me to show it to you in the dictionary, I'll pull out my Merriam-Webster and do just that. I trust that the editors and my professorial colleagues will not take offense.

1 Utah English Survey

Utahns have participated in a number of national and international dialect studies in the past. In a nationwide telephone survey,[1] data from only seven Utahns were collected, while the *Harvard Dialect Survey*[2] included 172 respondents from Utah. The *Cambridge Online Survey of World Englishes*[3] is an ongoing online survey that to date has gathered information on several hundred Utah residents, and while the results of the *Dialects of American English Survey*[4] are available, it is unclear how many Utahns participated.

Other surveys have focused solely on Utah. Some tested only one or two features of Utah English.[5] In contrast, Sarver and his team[6] interviewed 230 Utah residents, about half of whom had moved in from another state. He looked at five features. Lillie[7] carried out a survey of Utah English that contained responses from 732 participants. Her participants were asked about 42 different characteristics, which makes her survey the most comprehensive dialect study so far.

Much of the evidence I'm going to cite in the following chapters comes from a survey I carried out in 2020.[8] This chapter describes my survey in detail, and it may be a chapter you want to skip if you are just interested in the bottom line on Utah English. However, all the nitty-gritty is included here for the benefit of the hard-core linguists.

PARTICIPANTS

Initially 2,638 people signed on to the survey site, but many did not finish more than 15 percent of the survey's test items. I removed these incomplete data, as well as data from participants who were under 18 years of age, who had never lived in Utah, or who had completed the survey so quickly that they must have clicked through it rather than thoughtfully considered the

Table 1.1. Counties That Participants Were Raised in, or Presently
Reside in, and County Population

County	# Raised	# Residing	Population
Beaver	5	8	6,580
Box Elder	57	70	54,950
Cache	80	134	127,068
Carbon	26	24	20,269
Daggett	3	4	980
Davis	68	58	351,713
Duchesne	38	16	19,964
Emery	12	7	10,014
Garfield	28	29	5,080
Grand	19	21	9,764
Iron	55	8	52,775
Juab	41	70	11,555
Kane	5	134	7,709
Millard	40	24	13,006
Morgan	28	4	12,045
Piute	4	0	1,445
Rich	26	16	2,464
Salt Lake	165	7	1,152,630
San Juan	60	29	15,449
Sanpete	67	21	31,887
Sevier	54	8	21,539
Summit	17	70	41,933
Tooele	48	134	69,907
Uintah	26	24	35,438
Utah	205	4	622,213
Wasatch	52	58	33,240
Washington	44	16	171,700
Wayne	4	7	2,690
Weber	83	29	256,359
Multiple Counties	76		
Non-Utah	328	58	

questions. I also eliminated data from participants who responded incorrectly
to the attention-tester answers (see Test Item section). These omissions left
the data from 1,763 participants, 1,436 of whom were raised in Utah and 1,611
of whom presently reside in Utah. There were 1,282 participants who were
both raised and presently reside in the state.

Information about the counties in which the participants were raised and
reside appears in table 1.1 along with the total population of each county.[9] All

Table 1.2. Educational Attainment of Participants

Education	# Participants
2-Year Degree	213
4-Year Degree	488
Doctorate	269
High School Degree	238
Less Than High School	13
Some College	542
Total	1,763

Table 1.3. Religion of Participants

Religion	# Participants
Catholic	38
Evangelical	12
FLDS	3
CJCLDS (Nonpracticing)	267
CJCLDS (Practicing)	949
No Religion	381
Non-Christian	16
Other Christian	83
Protestant	14
Total	1,763

Utah counties were represented in the survey, something that no other study on Utah English has achieved. There were 1,261 female and 503 male participants who ranged in age from 18 to 86, with a mean age of 40.5. The participants had lived in Utah for an average 78.3 percent of their lives. Information on the participants' educational and religious backgrounds appears in tables 1.2 and 1.3.

TEST ITEMS

The survey included questions to test twenty-eight characteristics that are assumed to form part of Utah English (table 1.4). I chose these characteristics either because they have been the topic of previous research on Utah dialect, or because they are things that people often discuss as being Utah traits. Of course, there are many more than twenty-eight interesting things that may form part of Utah English, but some of them just can't be studied in a survey format. An example would be the supposedly unique Utah pronunciation of words like *mountain*. As you will see, in this book I discuss *mountain* and many other phenomena even though they were not tested in the survey.

Example questions for each of the characteristics, as well as details about how the responses were elicited and the kinds of responses elicited, appear in each corresponding section. In order to reduce the amount of time necessary to complete the survey, not all test items were seen by all participants,

Table 1.4. The 28 Characteristics and Phenomena Tested in the Survey and the Attention-Testing Questions

Characteristic/Phenomenon	Example
Pronounced [l]	*Balm:* [bɑm] or [bɑlm]
Fill/Feel Merger	*Meal:* m[i]l or m[ɪ]l
Fail/Fell Merger	*Jail:* j[eɪ]l or j[ɛ]l
Words Like *Measure*	*Treasure:* tr[eɪ]sure or tr[ɛ]sure
-day in Days of the Week	*Friday:* Frid[eɪ] or Frid[i]
Creek	*Creek:* cr[i]k or cr[ɪ]k
Roof	*Roof:* r[u]f or r[ʊ]f
Cord/Card Merger	*Cord:* c[o]rd[a] or c[ɑ]rd
Pin/Pen Merger	*Pin:* p[ɪ]n or p[ɛ]n
Beck/Bake Merger	*Beg:* b[ɛ]g or b[eɪ]g
Bag Raising	*Bag:* b[æ]g, b[ɛ]g, or b[eɪ]g
Pool/Pole/Pull Merger, [ul]	*School:* sch[u]l or other vowel
Pool/Pole/Pull Merger, [ʊl]	*Full:* f[ʊ]l or other vowel
Pool/Pole/Pull Merger, [ol]	*Goal:* g[o]l or other vowel
Hull/Hole/Hall Merger	*Hull:* h[ʌ]l or other vowel
Words Like *Laura*	*Laura:* L[ɑ]ra or L[o]ra
Tour	*Tour:* t[u]r or t[o]r
Alternatives to *You're Welcome,* mm-hmm, or uh huh	Use *mm-hmm,* or *uh huh* sometimes or never
Alternatives to *You're Welcome, You Bet*	Use *you bet* sometimes or never
Expressions for Takeout	*To stay or to go? Or For here or to go?*
Expressions for Next in Line	*I'll help who's next* or *I'll help whoever's next*
Pop, Soda, or *Coke*	*Pop, Coke, soda, soda pop,* or *soft drink*
Route as a Highway Name	*Route:* r[u]t or r[aʊ]t
Route Meaning "Path"	*Route:* r[u]t or r[aʊ]t
Route as a Verb	*Route:* r[u]t or r[aʊ]t
Propredicate *Do*	*Do you exercise regularly?: I ought to exercise, I ought to,* and *I ought to do.* Rate how likely you are to say it.
(Oh) *For* + Adjective	*You see an adorable puppy: How cute!, That's cute!,* or *For cute!* Rate how likely you are to say it.
Intrusive [t]	*Celsius:* celsius or cel**t**sius
Attention Tester, *bead*	*Bead:* b[i]d, b[o]d, or b[ɛ]d
Attention Tester, *rope*	*Rope:* r[o]pe, r[i]p, or r[ɑ]p

Phonetic symbols used in this table

[i] as in d**ee**p	[ʊ] as in l**oo**k	[ʌ] as in c**u**p
[eɪ] as in f**a**ke	[ɪ] as in s**i**t	[ɑ] as in f**a**ther
[ɛ] as in b**e**d	[æ] as in b**a**d	
[u] as in s**oo**n	[o] as in l**oa**d	

[a]In Western American English the vowels [o] and [ɔ] are not generally perceived as different. While it is true that [ɔ] appears before laterals and rhotics and [o] is used in other contexts, this distinction is not relevant to the discussion of vowel mergers before laterals. For this reason I chose not to distinguish these symbols in order to eliminate any confusion that it may cause some readers.

although some survey questions were. The total number of questions was ninety. I eliminated two of the questions because they contained errors, leaving eighty-eight questions. However, each participant answered only fifty-five of these. To achieve this smaller number of questions, I created two versions of the survey. Questions that were rated along a scale of *Very likely* to *Very unlikely* were converted into numbers for the analysis; those numbers were not seen by the participants. In addition to the relevant test items, I included a number of attention testers. Some were included as responses to valid questions, while two were included in questions designed only to assess attention to the task.

METHOD AND PROCEDURE

To recruit participants from all parts of the state, I joined 136 Reddit and Facebook groups that were dedicated to certain counties or cities. These groups included You know you're from Kanab when; Wayne County Rant; Gunnison Utah 24/7 Yard Sales; Wasatch County Open Forum; and This is our town Fairview, Utah. I initially asked the group moderators if they would consent to my solicitation. The majority of the responses I received from them were in the affirmative, but most did not bother to respond. If the moderators responded in the negative, I did not post. If I received no response, I posted the solicitation. Only two groups expressed annoyance that I had posted the solicitation. In some cases, to join a group it was necessary to answer questions about my relationship with the area and my purpose for joining. I answered that I was interested in the speech of people in that area, and that answer satisfied most group administrators.

Facebook initially banned me as a result of my activity but later reduced the penalty to a temporary ban on joining or posting on group sites. To my great relief, however, this ban did not result in the removal of the solicitation from the sites. I gathered all the data over a four-day period, which resulted in much rejoicing on my part. It seems that people responded when the solicitation appeared in a new post, but after more recent posts pushed my post to the bottom of the feed it received little attention.

I modified my solicitation for each group to include the city, county, or part of the state that the group served. The announcement included a graphic of the state with a large question mark and a cartoon figure looking pensive superimposed on top of the graphic. The solicitation read:

You can tell you are from LOCATION NAME if . . .
Some say people in LOCATION NAME have their own way of talking, and others say they talk like everyone else in Utah. If you're over 18 you can help us figure out what's true by taking this 8- to 12-minute survey (and if you like, be put in a drawing for one of four $50 Amazon gift certificates for finishing it!). You'll answer questions like whether you pronounce "cot" and "caught" the same or not.

LINK TO SURVEY
Be sure to forward this message to your friends and family, especially those in your area, but also to those in other parts of Utah.

I designed and carried out the survey using the Qualtrics presentation service. Upon logging into the survey, the participants were shown the following instructions:

You'll be asked to say a word like **ma**rry and decide if the highlighted part of **ma**rry sounds more like the highlighted part of **me**n, or **ma**n. We only care about how you perceive the relationship between the words, not how anyone else would say them. And it's not about how people may say that one answer is better than the other. That's completely ridiculous! It's as weird as saying that it's "better" to prefer Coke over Pepsi, or "more correct" to like hamburgers better than pizza. Everyone has their own style and preferences. We just want to know what yours are.

Participants were then asked to agree or disagree to a consent form, and they answered a number of biographical questions: age, biological gender, number of years lived in Utah, state or Utah county raised in, state or Utah county presently residing in, Utah county they spent the most time in, education level, and religion. At that point the participants were randomly assigned one of the two versions of the survey. The questions were presented in a random order, as were the responses.

Participants were given the option of providing their email address if they wanted to be included in the drawing for four $50 Amazon gift certificates, which were offered to encourage participation. I emphasized the fact that the email addresses would be kept separate from participant responses and would

Figure 1.1. Division of Utah counties into three regions. (Credit: Original unmodified map of Utah from https://commons.wikimedia.org/wiki/File:Map_of_Utah_highlighting_Emery_County.svg)

not be shared with anyone. I chose four winners at random and contacted them so that their certificates could be awarded.

Of course, the survey data came from Utahns, and because none of the data relates to people from other states, the question of how Utah compares to other states on these twenty-eight characteristics can't be evaluated. Nevertheless, the effect of the participant's age, gender, education (simplified in the analysis to high school or less versus some college), and how much of their life had been lived in Utah can all influence word use and pronunciation. In addition to these factors, the influence of the participants' religion can be determined. For the purposes of the study, religion was simplified to three values: practicing members of The Church of Jesus Christ of Latter-day Saints (CJCLDS), nonpracticing members of the CJCLDS, and members of other religions. If participants indicated no religion, they were classified as belonging to another religion. This was done for simplicity's sake, and other studies have found that these groups influence pronunciation in Utah and in other CJCLDS communities.[10]

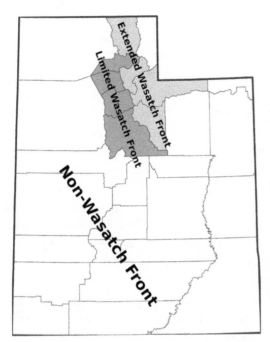

Figure 1.2. Division of counties into extended, limited, and non-Wasatch Front (the extended Wasatch Front includes the limited Wasatch Front). (Credit: Original unmodified map of Utah from https://commons.wikimedia.org/wiki/File:Map_of_Utah_highlighting_Emery_County.svg)

There were six variables for the county the person was raised in or resides in:

1. County Population: The population of the county.
2. Region: 3 Regions. North, Central, and South (figure 1.1).[11]
   North: Box Elder, Cache, Rich, Weber, Morgan, Tooele, Davis, Salt Lake, Utah, Wasatch, Summit, Duchesne, Daggett, Uintah.
   Central: Juab, Millard, Sanpete, Sevier, Carbon, Emery, Grand.
   South: Beaver, Piute, Wayne, Iron, Garfield, San Juan, Washington, Kane.
3. Region: Limited Wasatch Front (figure 1.2). Davis, Salt Lake, Utah, and Weber.
4. Region: Extended Wasatch Front includes the limited Wasatch Front (figure 1.2). Cache, Davis, Morgan, Salt Lake, Summit, Utah, Wasatch, and Weber.
5. Participants born and raised in Utah or not.
6. The individual county in which participants reside.

STATISTICAL ANALYSIS

I'll forewarn you that this section is dull and technical, and written principally for the language scholar, so many of you may want to skip ahead. In any event, a number of statistical analyses were used. Linear mixed-effects models were applied to data with continuous dependent variables. Binominal mixed-effects logistic regressions were carried out on data with a binary dependent variable. Test item was included as a random effect when there was more than one item per trait examined. When the participants provided more than one response to a question probing a particular pronunciation or phenomenon, participant was also included as a random effect. When there were no repeated measures, mixed-effects models were not necessary and fixed-effects only regression was carried out. All continuous variables such as age and percent of life spent in Utah were used in the statistical model, but these variables are presented as categorized variables in the graphs.

Jamovi,[12] which is a graphical user interface (GUI) for R software,[13] was used to carry out the analyses. Ordinal dependent variables, such as the rating scale of 2, 1, -1, -2, were treated as continuous. Least significant difference post hoc analyses were applied with a Bonferroni correction to test differences between the values of an independent variable. I discuss comparisons whose p values were .05 or smaller in the prose but don't include the numeric results of the post hoc tests, some of which would cover many pages. In order to gauge the effect strength of a particular predictor variable, I include the R^2 that resulted when each predictor was included by itself in the statistical model. These appear in the last column of the tables of the statistical results.

Because collinearity can cast doubt on the outcome of an analysis, I tested for collinearity between each pair of variables in each analysis. In analyses with numeric predictor variables, I carried out a linear regression with the numeric predictor compared to all other predictors and examined the variance inflation factor (VIF) to make sure it was under two. All categorical predictors were compared in a chi square test of association, and values of Cramer's V larger than .08 were considered to indicate collinearity. I don't provide the collinearity statistics in each analysis because none were found.

Many of the test responses had more than two values, and in some cases there were more than fifteen. This increased number of values occurred when the participants could choose from among five vowel choices and could also choose more than one vowel. It was possible to reduce the number of values by combining the less-common values into a single value called *other*. This combined value helped limit the number of values, but the analysis of these data required a multinomial logistic regression. However, a single multinomial logistic regression that included many independent variables and two random effects often required more than twenty-four hours to complete, which went beyond the threshold of my patience. The results of multinomial analyses are also difficult to interpret. For this reason, I chose to make binary groupings of the values of the dependent variable and run multiple binary regressions instead of a single multinomial analysis. For example, instead of carrying out one multinomial regression on a dependent variable with five values (e.g., [ʊ, u, ɑ, ʌ, o]), this could be reduced to different binary regressions, one with the values [ʊ] versus all other vowels, another with the values [u] versus all other vowels, and so on. This grouping also made interpreting the outcome more straightforward.

As I already discussed, the counties were grouped in a number of different arrangements. There are two reasons for choosing these combinations of counties. The first is that including every county in the statistical model often resulted in a model that did not converge. This occurred because some counties have few participants. In addition, in some smaller counties there is not a variety of people with different educational levels or different religions, for example, making it impossible to calculate the effect of each factor considered. The second reason is that, while differences between individual counties may be of interest, one principal purpose of this study is to determine how Utah is best divided into dialect regions, hence the different groupings of counties.

When running the statistics, I included each of the six combinations of county variables one at a time, and whichever combination produced the better fit was retained in the model. Continuous variables such as age and percent of life spent in Utah were standardized. For each of the characteristics examined, the most parsimonious model is reported. I arrived at this model by eliminating any variables that did not reach significance.

Interpreting the Statistical Results Using R^2

In addition to knowing what predictor variables were significant, we need to interpret the outcome of the survey in terms of how strongly a predictor is related to the phenomenon that was being tested. The statistical results include various measures of R^2: the R^2 of each predictor variable when it occurs

Table 1.5. R^2 Values from the Statistical Analysis of the *Cord/Card* Merger

Predictor	R^2
County of Residence	.437
Age	.007
Religion	.029
Education	.023

Marginal R^2 = .457
Conditional R^2 = .588

by itself in the model, the marginal R^2, and the conditional R^2. But, what does R^2 actually tell you? It's a measure of how much of the variance is accounted for. Say you weigh many different volumes of water. How much of the weight is accounted for by the volume? All of it. There is nothing else that influences the weight of the water except its volume. This experiment would result in an R^2 of 1.0, meaning that 100 percent of the variance in the weight of the water is accounted for by the volume of the water.

Now, what if you measured various volumes of different liquids besides water? The R^2 of volume would be smaller than 1.0 because volume by itself no longer accounts for all the variance in the weight; the type of liquid accounts for part of the variance besides the weight. If you added type of liquid as a predictor along with volume of liquid, the R^2 would once again reach 1.0. Very high R^2 values are not common when measuring human behavior because, unlike with inanimate objects such as water, there are so many things that we can't measure in people. These include a person's life experience, their mood, and so on.

Cohen[14] gave some general guides to interpreting R^2; values around .01 indicate a small effect size, those around .09 a medium effect size, and those above around .25 a large effect size. Let's look at the R^2 values from the *cord/card* merger that I'll present in chapter 5 (table 1.5). Using Cohen's guidelines, we can conclude that the county of residence has a large effect on the pronunciation of the vowel in words demonstrating the *cord/card* merger; it accounts for 43.7 percent of the variance. Religion and education have a small effect, while the R^2 for age is a minuscule .007. Although age is significantly related to this merger, it doesn't account for much of the variance in pronunciation, and it shows that the merger hasn't lost much ground over time.

The marginal R^2 indicates how much of the variance all of the predictor variables in the model account for, and in the model shown in table 1.5, it is 45.7 percent. If you add all of the R^2 values for each individual predictor variable together, the sum doesn't usually equal the marginal R^2 value, but it comes close. The difference has to do with the fact that the values are calculated in different models. What about the conditional R^2 of .588? It is higher than the marginal R^2 of .457, so it's telling us that some other variable is responsible for some of the variance.

I know there are two additional things that may account for part of the variance. The first is the individual test item. The four test items for the *cord/card* merger question were *cord, horse, Lord,* and *before.* I realize that there may be differences in the responses to these words, and I really don't care if more people matched *horse* to the vowel [ɑ] than they did *Lord.* That's why I included the test item as a special kind of variable called a random-effect variable. Second, I know that individual participants have their own way of speaking and their own personal idiosyncrasies. So, while I'm not interested in the fact that Joe matched more words with [ɑ] than Sally did, I do need to see how much of the variance individual differences have on the outcome, so participant was included as a random effect as well. The conditional R^2 (.588) is the amount of variance that the predictors account for, that is the marginal R^2 (.457) plus the variance that test items and test participants account for. A little subtraction gives you .131, which indicates that participants and test items account for 13.1 percent of the variance.

Why is this so important? Consider the results of the *fail/fell* merger question (chapter 5) in which the only significant variable was the region the person was raised in. The marginal R^2 of .003 indicates that this predictor accounts for only 0.3 percent of the variance, hardly anything. On the other side, the extremely high conditional R^2 of .956 reveals that 95.3 percent of the variance (.956−.003) is due to differences in the test items and the participants. The four test items—*bail, jail, rail,* and *tail*—received similar responses (11 percent, 18 percent, 18 percent, and 17 percent, respectively), so not a lot of the variance explained has to do with differences between test items. Instead, we can conclude that the explanation for the bulk of the variance to responses to the *fail/fell* merger questions resides in the speakers themselves. Some people merge, and others don't, and their individual behavior is not the result of where they were raised, or their gender, their religion, and so on.

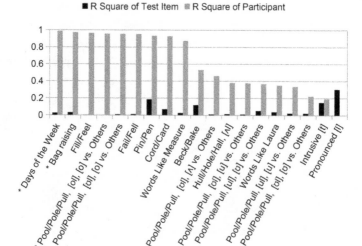

Figure 1.3. R^2 values for the random effects of test item and participant in each statistical analysis.

Figure 1.3 contains the R^2 values that show how much of the variance is accounted for by the test items and participants in each of the analyses presented in subsequent chapters. It should be clear that for many of these analyses the influence of test item and participant dominates that of the predictor variables. In fact, analyses marked with asterisks had no significant predictor variables associated with them. This is why it is crucial to consider the R^2 values when interpreting the results of the statistical analyses presented in this book.

Scone, Sluff, and Potato Bug

What Makes Utah Vocabulary Unique?

The idea that certain words are unique to Utah is popular and is often discussed in casual conversation, in online discussion groups, and in blogs, and it sometimes even makes its way into the media.[1] The problem is that much of the vocabulary people assume is unique to Utah speech really isn't. Let me explain why. It has to do with the *different-means-unique effect*. To illustrate this concept, consider the use of the term *toilet papering* to refer to the annoying act of covering the trees and bushes in someone's yard with toilet paper, a common teenage prank. Toilet papering isn't the only term for this quasi-vandalistic practice. The *Dialects of American English Survey*[2] indicates that the use of *toilet papering*—rather than *rolling, wrapping, TPing*, and so on—is most common in the shaded areas of the map in figure 2.1.

When a person from an unshaded area travels to or interacts with a person from Utah, a state that falls into the shaded area, and that person hears a Utahn use the term *toilet papering*, they correctly observe that this particular vocabulary item exists in Utah. The problem is that people often fall prey to the different-means-unique effect. This happens when they go a step further and incorrectly assume that because they have never heard the term except from a Utahn, it must exist in Utah and Utah alone even though it exists elsewhere too.

This is a fairly common phenomenon. For instance, Hanson[3] provides three examples of this error in one newspaper article. He cites the fact that in Utah, *caramel* is given two syllables (*carmel*) rather than three, yet this pronunciation is common throughout the country.[4] Another case he discusses is dropping the *r* in *library* so that the word is rendered *libary*. The internet is full of people decrying this pronunciation without specifically mentioning Utah—just google *libary, library pronunciation*. The month of *February* has suffered the same *r*-dropping fate, yet few Americans fail to drop the first *r* in casual conversation. We seem to be averse to having two *r*s so close together in words like

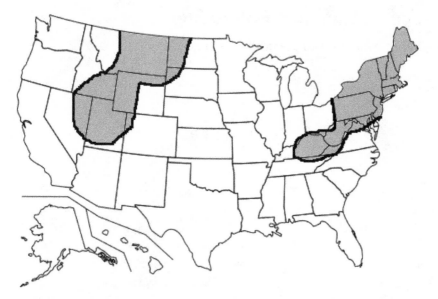

Figure 2.1. Regions where *toilet papering* is the most common term.(Credit: Original unmodified blank map of U.S. created by Kaboom88, public domain, https://commons .wikimedia.org/w/index.php?curid=2989307)

library and *February*. Finally, Hanson pegs pronouncing *-ing* as *-in'* on Utahns! Seriously? If there is something that occurs to some extent, in every single English speaker, in every area of the globe, across the centuries, it is this.

Another potential mistake of applying the different-means-unique effect is that those who do often assume that because one Utahn said *libary* or *toilet papering*, all Utahns, in every instance, and in all parts of the state, employ that term. Such false assumptions are simply due to limited data, and I realize that most people aren't linguists and aren't going to go to their local library in search of better evidence. For this reason, I want to examine some words that have been put forth as Utahisms, but really aren't, then move on to discuss words that may be bona fide, but not exclusively, Utahisms. The last part of the chapter looks at the results of my survey that deal with a number of words and expressions.

There are bucketloads of words that could be included in this chapter, but I have intentionally excluded two kinds of words. The first are words relating to place names. It's not really all that surprising that *Timp*, referring to Mount Timpanogos, is uncommon in other regions of the country; no place else has a Timp. In the same way, you don't expect the nicknames for universities in the state (i.e., *The U* and *The Y*) to be widely known outside of Utah. The frequency of words like these is more a matter of geography rather than linguistic diversity, and for that reason these words really aren't all that noteworthy.

The second category of words, which are often erroneously included in lists of Utahisms, are terms relating to The Church of Jesus Christ of Latter-day Saints (CJCLDS). Of course, you expect there to be vocabulary differences between the general public and members of particular religious organizations, but such differences are also found between the general public and the speech of people belonging to other groups, such as members of the military, steel workers, and professional musicians. About 62 percent of Utahns are members of the CJCLDS,[5] which makes words such as *ward*, meaning "congregation," more common in Utah. The problem is that those same words are just as common among English-speaking members who do not live in Utah. For this reason, you've got to consider these words more group-related than they are state-related, so they're not going to get any press here.

Some words may be flashes in the pan that may not have staying power. Take for example *lurpy* and its nominal counterpart *lurp*, meaning a socially awkward, uncoordinated, and nerdy person. I couldn't convince myself to include it in the body of this chapter. The term did make its way into some slang dictionaries,[6] and some online discussions associate it with Utah, but most don't. Many born-and-raised Utahns are unfamiliar with it as well. It appears to have popped up a few years ago just to fade out.

FINDING DISTINCTIVE UTAH VOCABULARY

How do you figure out if a word is a Utahism? Well, you could conduct a nationwide survey, which would be hard and expensive to do. However, in the past few decades the quantity of data available in electronic form has increased exponentially. At one point, the internet search giant Google set the lofty goal of digitizing every book ever published, and by 2015 they had scanned 30 million volumes.[7] But, Google must have realized that they bit off more than they could chew, because it appears they have put that project on the back burner. Nevertheless, linguists, who use collections of texts to conduct their investigations, saw the enormous potential for using Google's digitized texts to explore questions about language as well.

Table 2.1. Corpora Used in the Study

Acronym	Corpus Name	Corpus Size	Reference
BNC	*British National Corpus*, BYU Interface	100 million	Davies 2004
COCA	*Corpus of Contemporary American English*	560 million	Davies 2008
COHA	*Corpus of Historical American English*	400 million	Davies 2010
iWeb	*iWeb Corpus*	14 billion	Davies 2018
TV	*TV Corpus*	325 million	Davies 2019
Movies	*Movie Corpus*	200 million	Davies 2019
GloWbE	*Corpus of Global Web-based English*	1.9 billion	Davies 2013
Google Books	*Google Books Corpus*, BYU Interface	unknown	Davies 2011

Of course, the internet itself is a vast corpus, but it just doesn't allow users to search for the kinds of things that linguists are interested in, such as what words begin with *un-*, or what nouns follow the verb *walk*. For this reason, a number of linguistics-friendly collections of documents have been created. The ones I'll use were created by Mark Davies. These collections of texts are called corpora (or corpus in the singular; it's one of those funny plurals English got from Latin, like *datum/data* or *index/indices*). I'll use the corpora in table 2.1 to investigate certain words and their relationship to Utah, and I will refer to the corpora by their acronyms, which are included in the table.

Biff

Scribner[8] cites *biff*, meaning "to crash or make a mistake," as the top slang word in Utah. What makes this claim a bit suspicious from the outset is that the data Scribner based it on came from a survey of 2,000 people carried out by an online gambling site. What the heck? Furthermore, it is unclear exactly how the survey was conducted. I dug deeper into information about the word and found that the Oxford English Dictionary[9] defines the verb *to biff* as "to hit or strike" and shows that this meaning was attached to the word as far back as the late nineteenth century. But wait, there's more. The online crowdsourced Urban Dictionary,[10] created in the first decade of the twenty-first century, gives these as definitions: "fall hard, mess up, wipe out, make a mistake." It looks like the meaning of *biff* has expanded in the last hundred years. It went from "dealing a blow to another person or object," to "dealing a blow to oneself in either a literal or figurative manner."

Biff is definitely not a new word, but the question is whether its semantic expansion is limited to the speech of Utahns or if its usage is of a more general nature. The Corpus of Contemporary American English[11] contains numerous references to bikers and skiers crashing or *biffing it*, and few of these references have any demonstrable relationship to Utah. In the TV Corpus,[12] *biff* is also used to mean "mess up, make a mistake," as the following examples from that corpus illustrate.

1. We already biffed the Kanye and Rihanna album releases.
2. It all started because I lost a huge bag of cocaine, so I totally biffed it.
3. I know you biffed it with the kids yesterday.
4. Guys!—Are you okay?—Biff that one.—You biffed it?
5. I really hope he biffs it like he usually does.[13]

Now, given the number of ski runs and bike trails in Utah, *biffing it* may be a more common occurrence in Utah compared to other states, but the fact that it appears in the speech of many people and many TV characters who are unrelated to the Beehive State suggest that *biff* is a term whose use is generalized in American English. Sorry folks, it's not a Utahism.

(Ride) shotgun

DeBry[14] claims that the expression *to ride shotgun*, meaning "to occupy the seat next to the driver," is not unique to Utah but that it originated there. The basis for the claim is an article that is purportedly the earliest reference to the expression. It was published in May 1919 in the *Ogden Examiner*.[15] One problem with this evidence is that it incorrectly assumes that the place something is first documented is necessarily the same place where it originated. What's more, the Oxford English Dictionary[16] cites an earlier 1912 reference to *riding shotgun* from *Cosmopolitan*, and further investigation may reveal even earlier instances, none of which would necessarily lead us closer to the origin of the phrase.

According to the Google Books Corpus,[17] references to *ride/rode/riding shotgun* are actually quite scarce early on. There are few cases prior to the 1930s, when 22 references are registered. From that decade on, the phrase begins a steady climb, continuing into the twenty-first century when there are 3,877 references. The reason for the mounting popularity of the phrase is most likely that it was popularized by its use in Hollywood cowboy westerns, as DeBry claims. Once again, there is no substantive link to a Utah origin for *riding shotgun*. Dang it.

Sluff (Slough) School

Sluff, meaning "skip class," is one of the most often cited vocabulary items that are purported to be uniquely Utahn.[18] The alternate spelling *slough* is also cited as a Utah usage in the Dictionary of Regional American English.[19] A search of the iWeb Corpus,[20] which contains 14 billion words from the six largest English-speaking countries, reveals only three instances of *sluff* and *sluffing* (and their variants *slough* and *sloughing*) that refer to truancy. Two of them are from Utah sources, and one is from southern Idaho, an area that shares many linguistic traits with Utah:

1. A truancy letter may be issued to a student for sluffing.
2. Attend class every day. (She would not tolerate any sluffing).
3. Students who sluff an assembly will receive the same punishment as if they had sluffed a class.[21]

No cases of *sluff* were found in COCA, TV, Movie Corpus, or Corpus of Global Web-based English. However, a search of the internet with the Google search engine yielded numerous cases of *sluff* related to Utah. For example, the term was employed in a blog written by a Utah author. A handful of instances were identified from neighboring states as well:

4. I can never remember sloughing school.
5. Another man thought sluffing school would be at an all-time high because of the variety of things to do in the summer.[22]

Two cases of *slough school* appear in a word map of the eastern section of Nevada, the side that butts up against Utah.[23]

There is sporadic evidence that this vocabulary item is not completely unique to Utah and surrounding states. For example, Gardner R. Dozois, an author born in Salem, Massachusetts, used it in one of his novels.[24] Anecdotal reports of it have come from Southern California and Texas as well. However, the most convincing evidence that *sluff* is principally a Utahism is the results of the *Dialects of American English Survey*.[25] This is an online survey

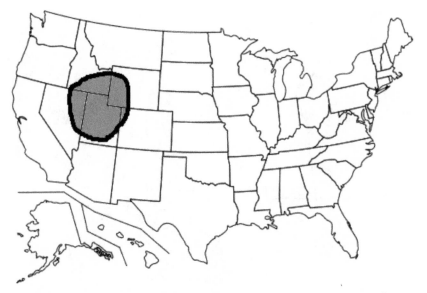

Figure 2.2. Where *sluff*, meaning "skip school," is a frequent choice in the Dialects of American English Survey. (Credit: Original unmodified blank map of U.S. created by Kaboom88, public domain, https://commons.wikimedia.org/w/index.php?curid=2989307)

in which participants were shown pictures of objects, or were given definitions of things, and asked to choose what word they would use from among several options. The origin of the speaker and the frequency of each response appears as a heat map. In the United States, various terms are used for truancy: *play hookey*, *skip school*, *bag school*, and *sluff school*. A modified version of the heat map for the outcome of *sluff school* appears in figure 2.2.[26]

These survey results clearly corroborate the notion that Utah is the focal point for *sluff*. They also demonstrate that this term overflows the borders of Utah into neighboring states, just as the corpus data indicate. Unlike *shotgun* and *biff*, *sluff* appears to be a true, but not unique, Utahism.

Potato Bug

Three different creatures are referred to by the name *potato bug*. One is a type of cricket (Stenopelmatus) also known as a *Jerusalem cricket*. The second is a type of beetle (*Leptinotarsa decemlineata*) that is often called a *Colorado potato beetle*. The third is a type of crustacean (Armadillidiidae) that in the United

Figure 2.3. Where armadillidiidae are called *potato bugs*. (Credit: Original unmodified blank map of U.S. created by Kaboom88, public domain, https://commons.wikimedia.org/w/index .php?curid=2989307)

States goes by various other names such as *pill bug* and *roly poly*. These critters have a hard gray shell and roll into a ball when disturbed. It is the reference to this creature as *potato bug* that I'm discussing in this section.

Unfortunately, cases of *potato bugs* in the corpora are useless for determining whether this term is particular to Utah, because in most instances it is unclear which creature is being referred to. Fortunately, one of the questions in the *Dialects of American English Survey*[27] asked the participants to name a picture of an Armadillidiidae. The results of that survey item show that these creatures are clearly known as *potato bugs* in Utah (figure 2.3).

What is intriguing about this map is not that Utah is highlighted but that other small areas of Ohio and New York are highlighted as well. The Church of Jesus Christ of Latter-day Saints began in Palmyra, New York, and was officially founded in 1830 in Fayette, New York. Both of these cities fall inside of *potato bug* zones. Religious intolerance drove members of the church from upstate New York to Kirtland, Ohio, beginning in 1831; northern Ohio is another *potato bug* area. The fact that the vast majority of the United States uses another term, such as *roly poly* or *pill bug*, suggests that use of the less-common term *potato bug* in Utah may have originated along the southern shores of Lakes Erie and Ontario. The distribution of *potato bug* in the United States serves as very plausible evidence that *potato bug* as a Utahism is traceable to nineteenth-century migration patterns.

What about the existence of *potato bug* in Washington and Oregon? The Oregon Trail was the major path of immigration to the Pacific Northwest in the latter half of the nineteenth century. The trail passed through southwest Wyoming and the Snake River Valley in Idaho, both of which are now within the *potato bug* zone. What's more, Salt Lake City was the only significant settlement in the region at that time. Many immigrants bound for the Northwest diverged from their path in order to take the Salt Lake/Hensley cutoff to Salt Lake City.[28] There the travelers would resupply with provisions and livestock before rejoining the trail and continuing their journey. Now, taking the cutoff entailed a 360-mile detour. Is it possible that enough of the Oregon Trail pioneers took this detour and had sufficient interaction with *potato bug* users that they would pick up the word and carry it to the Northwest? Is it possible that the pioneers who didn't take the Hensley cutoff learned it from people living in the sparsely populated areas of Wyoming and Idaho? These are interesting ideas, but I doubt there was enough sustained contact with other people for immigrants to pick up that vocabulary item on their way to the Northwest. Another explanation is warranted. Any takers?

Water Skeeter

The insects sometimes known as water skeeters are particularly fascinating for their ability to walk on water, a feat that gives them the name *Jesus bug* in some places. Biologists call them Gerridae, but common folk have quite a few different terms for them: *waterbug, waterstrider, water spider, skimmer, water beetle, pond skater, water skipper, water skater,* and *water skeeter.* The *Harvard Dialect Survey*[29] presented a picture of a Gerridae to people and asked them which of five words they used to refer to this creature. *Waterbug* was the most common answer (45 percent), but 22 percent of the survey takers knew of no word for them and 3 percent used a word other than the ones they were asked to choose from: *waterbug, backstrider, waterstrider, strider, water-spider, water crawler, skimmer,* or *water beetle.* Conspicuously absent from this list is *water skeeter.*

The *Dialects of American English Survey*[30] also included Gerridae as a test item, but like the *Harvard Dialect Survey,* failed to include *water skeeter* as

Figure 2.4. Places where people said they use another word to refer to Gerridae, which may be *water skeeter*. (Credit: Original unmodified blank map of U.S. created by Kaboom88, public domain, https://commons.wikimedia.org/w/index.php?curid=2989307)

a possible response. However, some respondents indicated that they used another term for the insect that was not included on the survey. When those other responses are mapped, they fall in an area that includes Utah and parts of other states to the north (figure 2.4).

To investigate this mystery more thoroughly, I searched for *water skeeter* through billions of words in the COCA, iWeb, TV, Movies, GloWbE, and Google Books corpora and found zilch. Googling the internet for the term provided numerous references to a pontoon boat that was once manufactured by a company in Stockton, California, that bore the name *Water Skeeter*, but I found nothing that could tie the word in with the state of Utah. Finally, I verified my suspicion that most of the survey respondents who said they had another term for the bug called it a *water skeeter*. The *Cambridge Online Survey of World Englishes*[31] did include *water skeeter* as a test choice, and although the use of this term could be found scattered throughout the western United States, *water skeeter* was definitely common in Utah. I'd conclude that that's enough evidence to place Z among the Utahisms.

Scone

While visiting London I once stopped into a pastry shop. Actually, I stopped into pastry shops many times during my trip which the bathroom scale attested to when I arrived home. In any event, I noticed a pastry with a card in front of it that said "Scone." It certainly didn't look anything like what I thought scones were.

The Oxford English Dictionary[32] notes that the word *scone* is of Scottish origin and defines it as "a large round cake made of wheat or barley-meal baked on a griddle." For most English speakers, *scone* refers to the baked variety. In the United States, this kind of bread is more likely to be called a biscuit. However, if you order a *scone* in a Utah restaurant, what you'll get is deep-fried bread dough. There are a few other terms for this kind of food in the United States. The most general one is *fry bread*. If served with Mexican cuisine it is a *sopaipilla*. In Native American contexts it is *Navajo fry bread* regardless of the tribal affiliation of the cook (and much to the chagrin of the non-Navajo cooks).

The word *scone* referring to fry bread is the alleged Utah term, but there is no mention of it as such in either the Urban Dictionary or the Dictionary of Regional American English. Unfortunately, it does not appear as a survey item in the *Dialects of American English Survey*.[33] Of course, there are numerous cases of *scone* in the corpora, but there's no way you can determine whether they refer to the baked or fried variety. However, internet searches for images of *Utah scones* and *Mormon scones* invariably depict the fried version, and internet discussions of the topic indicate that *scones* in Utah are not the kind of *scones* one would find elsewhere.

Census figures indicate that Utah has the highest concentration of English ancestry in the United States.[34] Given this fact, Eliason[35] suggests that it was this massive British immigration that solidly established the word *scone* in the state. Furthermore, he argues that the fried nature of the *scone* could be due, in part, to contact with Mexican *sopaipillas* as well as *Navajo fry bread*. The fact that Utah scones are fried rather than baked is most likely a matter of early frontier life, in which flour and lard were staples and a frying pan was much more available than an oven.

To complicate matters a bit, there is a hint that the fried version of the *scone* is not a Utah innovation after all. The Oxford English Dictionary[36] notes that one variety of *scone* is the *fried scone*, "one in which the ingredients are made into a batter and fried." Whether the fried version was brought with the

British immigrants or whether frying was a pioneer innovation, what makes *scones* unique in Utah, and what distinguishes them from *scones* in the rest of the country, is that they are deep fried and taste so good when smothered with butter and honey. *Scone* meaning "fry bread" is the closest thing to a truly unique word in the vocabulary of Utah.

Flipper Crotch

A *flipper crotch* or *flipper crutch* is a kind of slingshot. The Dictionary of American Regional English[37] cites this term as one used in the Rocky Mountains, especially in Utah, and the evidence bears this out. A few cases appear on a dialect map of eastern Nevada,[38] and the word is used by authors such as Wistisen,[39] who resides in Idaho, yet this just shows that characteristics of Utah English spill across state boundaries.

Now, if you ask a Utahn what a *flipper crotch* is, you'll probably be met with a blank stare. Few people are familiar with this word, for two reasons. The first is that people nowadays just don't own, use, or talk about *slingshots*, let alone *flipper crotches*, anymore. But, if you are lucky enough to encounter a Utahn who does know what a *flipper crotch* is, chances are they belong to the older generation. This is evident by the age of a number of Utah authors who use the term in their writing: Roger Ladd Memmott, born 1944;[40] Afton Lovell (Pettegrew) Wilkins, born 1932;[41] Kathryn Richards Sorensen, born 1926.[42] Apparently the art of fabricating and using *flipper crotches* simply did not get passed down to the next generation, and neither did the term. Words such as *gal*, *groovy*, and *swell* have suffered a similar fate with the passing of time.

Culinary Water

In contrast to *irrigation water*, *culinary water* is suitable for human consumption. The more common term for this is *potable water*. Although the Dictionary of Regional American English[43] cites *culinary water* as a usage common to Utah, I've never had anyone from out of state slap me on the wrist for using it or make me feel that the term is stigmatized. It appears to have escaped notice in media stories and internet discussions of Utah English as well.

The corpora tell a different story. The iWeb[44] contains seventy-four instances of *culinary water*, of which fifty-three refer to Utah, two to Ohio, and one to Nevada; the remaining eighteen are of indeterminate origin. The

Corpus of Historical American English[45] contains only one case, and that one mentions El Paso, Texas. Fourteen cases appear in the Corpus of News on the Web,[46] eleven of which refer to Utah, one to Pakistan, and two have an indeterminate reference. This evidence is certainly enough to demonstrate that *culinary water* is not unique to Utah. It does seem to be much more common there, but more evidence is needed to establish this as a fact.

One way to roughly estimate the frequency of *culinary water* in each state is to search the internet for the term along with a state name. Of course, this method has definite flaws, the first being that the Google search engine provides only an estimate about the frequency of the term in its databases, and that estimate is based on the number of pages containing a search term, not the actual number of instances of the term in question, which may appear many times in a single page. The other issue with this search is that the term and state name may appear on a document unrelated to the state. For example, a reference to *culinary water* and Colorado may reference the Colorado River, not the state of Colorado. In spite of these inherent difficulties, I obtained the frequency of *culinary water* and each state name using Google. Utah topped the list at 72,200 instances followed by Washington (22,800), which included the capital city as well as the state, and Massachusetts (19,900). Because more populous states arguably produce more documents, I divided the raw frequencies resulting from the search by the population in each state. When this is done, Utah again tops the list at .022 references per capita, followed by Montana (.016) and Wyoming (.013). All of this data suggests that *culinary water* is more commonly used in Utah but is not exclusive to that state.

So, the question is, Where did this term come from? The evidence suggests that it's not an Americanism. The Google Books Corpus[47] indicates the use of *culinary water* to refer to drinking water in numerous nineteenth-century British documents. The following are some examples:

1. The unhappy inhabitants have to seek culinary water from the ditches.
2. This warmth and lightness are increased by the heated culinary water which is poured down the drains.
3. To bring its culinary water from the western neighbourhoods of Siptitz Height.[48]

It appears, however, that *culinary water* hasn't stuck around in the UK because it's not very common in contemporary British English. For example, there are no instances of *culinary water* in the British National Corpus,[49] which is based on data from the last two decades of the twentieth century. In contrast, I found eleven instances of *potable water* there. What's more, a search of the internet using Google uncovered only 185 instances of the term in the domain .uk. This all suggests that *culinary water* has fallen out of use in the UK in the past one hundred years or so. What we have, then, is a case of a word of British origin that migrated to the United States and then fell out of common usage in the UK. In the United States, on the other hand, it is still used, but principally in Utah, the state with the most English influence.[50] For this reason, I think it's fair to say that *culinary water* is the result of the large numbers of people who immigrated from England to Utah, and it deserves an entry in the lexicon of Utah English.

Fork

A person from out of state who is traveling through Utah County is sure to wonder what nationalities and silverware have to do with the towns of Spanish Fork and American Fork. Is there a German Spoon or Chinese Knife nearby as well? The truth is that both American Fork and Spanish Fork were named after the rivers that run through them, and it is tempting to interpret *fork* to mean a fork in the river. However, the Spanish Fork and American Fork rivers aren't branches, tributaries, or forks of another river. In this case, how did they get their names, and what does *fork* mean? This term is related to the most salient feature of the state of Utah, which is its mountains. The landscape of a mountain is comprised of higher portions called peaks, ridges, and crests, while the lower parts are known as canyons, ravines, gulches, and draws. In Utah, these depressed areas were also called *forks*, and in Utah, as well as in other parts of the West, this name was applied regardless of whether a river runs through the area.

I looked for this particular definition of *fork* in the dictionary of all dictionaries, the Oxford English Dictionary, and it just wasn't there. This absence tells me that the use of *fork* with this meaning is particular to the western United States. The United States Geological Survey[51] contains 1,114 place names in Utah that contain *fork* (e.g., Henry's Fork, Diamond Fork, Dry Fork, Church Fork, Blacks Fork, Broad's Fork). Many of these places indeed contain streams, while others are parks, cities, trails, or locales named after streams. However, 331 of the place names are the names of valleys—in other words, *forks*. Beyond its use in place names, the word *fork* doesn't appear to be employed anymore

Table 2.2. Test Questions and Responses for Asking about Takeout

Test Question	Test Responses
Imagine you are working in a fast-food place. Someone places their order and you need to find out if they are going to take the food with them or if they are going to eat it in the restaurant. What would you ask them?	A *For here or to take?* (Attention tester) B *To stay or to go?* C *For here or to go?*

by present-day Utahns to mean "canyon" or "valley." For this reason, I'd tag it as a historical Utah term that has fallen out of productive use.

HOW VOCABULARY USAGE VARIES IN UTAH

Expressions for *Takeout*

When you place an order at a fast-food establishment, your server needs to know whether to put your food on a tray, because you will be eating at the restaurant, or to put it in a bag, because you are taking the food with you. Servers usually ask about your intentions in one of two common ways: *For here or to go?* or, *To stay or to go?* In a survey of about 100,000 people,[52] 12 percent said they used the phrase *to stay or to go*, while the remaining 88 percent preferred *for here or to go*. Which phrase is used where is the topic of many an internet discussion. Some people believe that *to stay or to go* is strictly a New York City thing.[53] Others note its use in Eastern Canada[54] and, of course, in Utah.[55]

In the survey I created, 63 percent of the Utahns chose *for here or to go* and 37 percent *to stay or to go*. So, using *to stay or to* go is definitely more common in the state, and since there is variation in its use, it would be nice to know what factors influence whether people ask *To stay or to go?* or *For here or to go?* By the way, in the survey there was a third option to choose from, *For here or to take?*, which was included as an attention tester. Because no one actually says this (I googled it), anyone who chose that response was probably just clicking through the survey without paying attention, which prompted me to eliminated all of their answers from further consideration.

The statistical analysis reveals a number of factors that influence whether someone is a *to stay or to go* or a *for here or to go* person (table 2.3). Please

Table 2.3. Statistical Results for Takeout Expressions

Predictor	χ^2	df	p	R^2
Age	22.3	1	< .001	.007
Percent of Life in Utah	33.9	1	< .001	.035
Gender	21.9	1	< .001	.009
Region Raised In—3 Regions	14.9	4	0.005	.029
Region of Residence—3 Regions	20.8	3	< .001	.019

McFadden's R^2 = .080

keep in mind that the R^2 gives you a sense of how strongly each of the factors contributes to the use of the expressions. Age, percent of life in Utah, county raised in, and county of residence all fall around .01, indicating a small effect of these predictors. Gender and age have much smaller R^2, which tells you that they exert only a modicum of influence. Medium-size influences fall around .09, and large ones around .25 or greater.

Although the survey notes that *for here or to go* is more frequently used, I believe that the older expression is *to stay or to go*. First, the use of *to stay or to go* increases for people who have spent more time in Utah, while those who have spent a smaller percentage of their lives in Utah tend to use *for here or to go* more often (figure 2.5). Second, older people prefer *to stay or to go* more than younger Utahns do (figure 2.6). The relationship between people's preferred term and their age may signal that there is a change in progress—that *for here or to go* is slowly ousting the older *to stay or to go*. This theory is corroborated by the fact that people who have spent less time in the state preferred *to stay or to go* less often than did longtime residents. As far as gender is concerned, women preferred the older *to stay or to go* more than men did (figure 2.7). According to Labov, in general, women tend to prefer more "prestigious" (in other words, what people consider "correct") speech,[56] so their preference for *to stay or to go* may indicate that this expression is more prestigious in Utah.

When I ran the statistics, I tried different groupings of the counties according to where the participants were raised or reside,[57] and I report the results of the best-fitting group. The data point to some regional differences in the use of each takeout expression when the state is divided into thirds. The chart in figure 2.8 illustrates the variation according to the part of the state that the participants were raised in. When each area is compared to every other

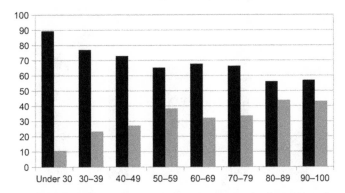

Figure 2.5. Percent of responses to the takeout question by percent of life spent in Utah.

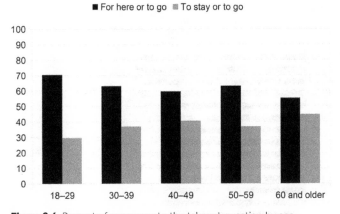

Figure 2.6. Percent of responses to the takeout question by age.

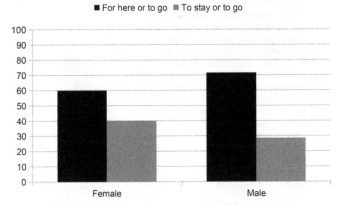

Figure 2.7. Percent of responses to the takeout question by gender.

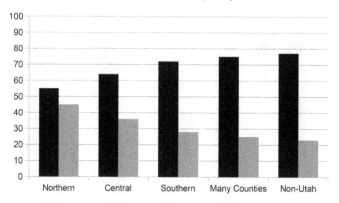

Figure 2.8. Percent of responses to the takeout question by the region the participants were raised in.

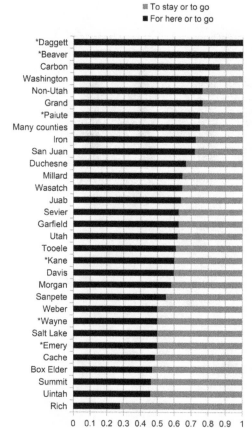

Figure 2.9. Proportion of responses to the takeout question by the county the participants were raised in.

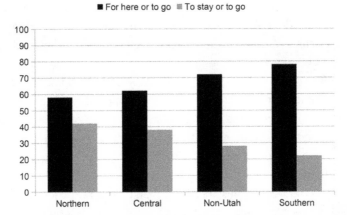

Figure 2.10. Percent of responses to the takeout question by the present residence of the participants.

area, participants raised in the southern counties don't differ statistically from any other group. However, those raised in the northern third of the state prefer *to stay or to go* more than those raised in the central part do, and more than those raised in many different counties do. Participants raised outside of Utah preferred *to stay or to go* less often than those raised in many counties and those raised in the central portion of the state.

The proportion of responses in each county may be of interest to some. This information appears in figure 2.9. Counties with fewer than ten participants are marked with an asterisk; when there are few participants it is difficult to assume that their responses are a good estimate of the entire county, so this graph should be interpreted with that caveat in mind.

Also relevant is which third of the state (i.e., northern, central, and southern) the participants presently reside in (figure 2.10). When those regions are compared to each other statistically, they reveal a great deal. The regions can basically be reduced to two: southern Utah and everyplace else. That is, residents of northern Utah and central Utah, along with Utahns not presently living in the state, group together because their preference for the takeout terms don't differ significantly. At the same time, all three of those groups differ from southern Utah. So, it's safe to say that *for here or to go* is much more likely to be used by Utah's southerners than by those in the rest of the state, although both expressions are to be found no matter where you are in Utah.

There is a tempting explanation for why *for here or to go* dominates in southern Utah. The bulk of the population there lives in the St. George area. More specifically, Washington County contains the St. George area and houses 65 percent of the residents of southern Utah. St. George is one of the fastest-growing cities in the nation; in fact, in 2018 it was at the top of the list.[58] The growth is not due to a major baby boom there since St. George is known as a retirement community. The city's population is skyrocketing because of the number of people moving in. Although I couldn't find solid evidence for it, my guess is that many of those flocking to red rock country are not Utahns and that they are bringing their *for here or to go* with them. However, this explanation is suspect because northern Utah has also experienced an influx of residents from other states, yet it does not pattern with southern Utah with respect to expressions for takeout.

Alternatives to *You're Welcome*

When you were a kid, you probably learned to say *thank you* when you were given something and to say *you're welcome* if someone thanked you. My best guess is that no one taught you to say *mm-hmm* or *you bet* when you were thanked, yet those are common responses heard from some, but not all, Utahns.

Just who are the *mm-hmm* people? I asked this question in my survey (see table 2.4), and 63 percent of respondents recognized saying *mm-hmm* or *uh huh* some of the time; 37 percent indicated that they never do. The statistics show that it depends on age.[59] As figure 2.11 illustrates, younger people were more likely to mark that they sometimes say *mm-hmm* or *uh huh* much more than older people, who felt that they never use those responses.

Table 2.4. Test Questions and Responses for the Variants of *You're Welcome*

Test Question	Test Responses
When someone says "thank you" it's common to respond "you're welcome." Do you say "uh huh" or "mm-hmm" to mean "you're welcome"?	A Sometimes B Never
When someone says "thank you" it's common to respond "you're welcome." Do you say "you bet" to mean "you're welcome"?	A Sometimes B Never

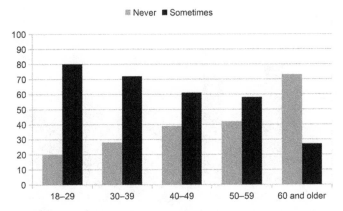

Figure 2.11. Percent of *mm-hmm/uh huh* for *you're welcome* answers by age.

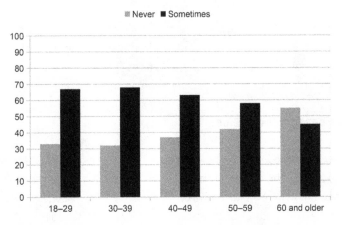

Figure 2.12. Percent of *you bet* for *you're welcome* answers by age.

What about *you bet*? In her survey, Lillie[60] asked people how to respond to *thank you*, and 2.5 percent of them answered *you bet*. In my survey, 62 percent of the participants responded that they sometimes use *you bet*, while 38 percent said they never do. The use of *you bet* is not only related to age but also depends on what part of the state the person was raised in.[61] Younger people were more likely to recognize that they sometimes say *you bet* than older people were (figure 2.12).

When each regional group is compared with every other group (figure 2.13), the only significant differences are that participants raised in central Utah

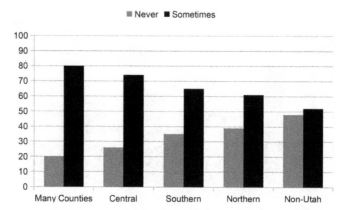

Figure 2.13. Percent of *you bet* for *you're welcome* answers by the region the participants were raised in.

recognized that they say *you bet* more often than respondents from the northern third of the state or those not raised in the state. The age data suggest an apparent time change, meaning that *mm-hmm, uh huh,* and *you bet* are not going anywhere and may even become more popular in the future.

Expressions for *Next in Line*

If you've ever stood in a long line in a coffee shop, you have certainly heard the server call out to the person at the head of the line, *Can I help who's next?* The self-appointed grammar police who post online have had a heyday condemning this expression as slothful, uneducated, and likely to lead to the downfall of the English language as we know it if not held in check. However, this phrase is not particularly Utahn. One speculation is that it started in the upper Midwest,[62] but it's not an Americanism because it's been heard in southern England as well.[63]

Generally, when people hear an expression that they brand as having bad grammar, they assume that it's a newfangled corruption of the proper way of speaking. That is to say, they speculate that *whoever* in *Can I help who's next?* has been shortened to *who* out of laziness. Actually, the opposite is true. Linguists consider *who's next* an example of a fused relative construction. Fused relatives aren't new constructions; they are actually quite old and were thought to have gone extinct more than a hundred years ago.[64] If you examine older documents, you'll see that their authors used *who* in many places where writers using contemporary English prefer *whoever.* For example, take a line from the

Table 2.5. Test Question and Responses for *Who's/Whoever's Next*

Test Question	Test Responses
If you are serving people who are standing in line, how would you call to the next person in line?	A *I'll help who's next* B *I'll help whoever's next*

Bard himself (that's English majors' nickname for Shakespeare). He put these words into one of his character's mouths: *Who steals my purse steals trash.*[65] Now that wording probably grates many people's ears nowadays, most of whom would prefer *whoever* over *who*. So, it seems that this old-fashioned fused relative construction didn't become extinct altogether but somehow survived long enough to have undergone a minor renaissance, at least in the question *Can I help who's next?*

To examine the wording of this question in Utah, I included the question in a survey item (see table 2.5). The responses were about 50-50 (51 percent *whoever's*; 49 percent *who's*). The only difference that jumped out of statistical analysis was where the participant was raised.[66] To compare results from each of Utah's regions, I performed a post hoc analysis. It revealed what is evident in figure 2.14. Utahns who live outside of the limited Wasatch Front use *who's next* more often than people who don't presently live in Utah as well as Utahns who do live in the limited Wasatch Front. Taken together, this information indicates that *who's next* is more commonly found among people who live in

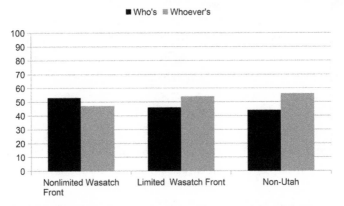

Figure 2.14. Preference for *who's next* and *whoever's next* by the region the participant was raised in.

the rural areas of the state. Unfortunately, the survey didn't give us any clues about the direction these expressions are likely to go in the future.

CONCLUSIONS

Perhaps the most difficult part of writing this chapter was deciding what words or expressions to include or exclude. I included *biff* and *ride shotgun* as examples of words erroneously associated with Utah, but others weren't so easy to choose. New words, or new definitions of old words, continually pop up. It is hard to determine which ones become regionalisms because many fade away as quickly as they appear. Other terms hang on only in the older generations and aren't passed on to the younger folks. *Flipper crotch* fits nicely into this category. It was definitely a term used principally in Utah, but it will probably be taken to the grave with those who know what it means. In like manner, the term *fork*, meaning ravine or canyon, has already been taken to the grave. While it still appears in Utah and the western United States, it has died in contemporary speech, and is now conserved only in place names.

There are a few expressions I included even though they are very frequent outside of Utah. One of these is the takeout question, *To stay or to go?* Another is, *Can I help who's next?* Because some people associate these phrases with Utah English, I wanted to get a sense of their place in the state. Using *mm-hmm* and *you bet* in place of *you're welcome* fit in this category as well. These responses are interesting because they appear to be catching on among younger Utahns, but we need some comparative data from other states to get a better sense of the extent to which these are Utah characteristics.

However, I'll vouch for *culinary water* as a Utah term. While its roots go back to the UK, and although it exists in other regions of the United States, the term appears to be much more frequent in Utah than elsewhere. Along the same lines, *potato bug* and *water skeeter* are the most prevalent terms for these creatures in the state, although the terms do exist in other small pockets of the country as well.

So, is there any word or expression that is truly a Utahism? The expression *sluff school* comes very close—it is extremely rare outside Utah and southern Idaho. The one lexical item that I can find no reference to outside of Utah, and which seems to be the only true and unique vocabulary item in the state, would have to be *scone*, meaning fried bread dough.

For Cute and Used to Do

Utah Grammatical Novelties

3

OH, FOR CUTE!: (OH) FOR + ADJECTIVE

Origin of (Oh) For + Adjective

I have a cousin who, when we were growing up, would exclaim, "Oh, for cute!" whenever she came across a cuddly puppy. This expression probably strikes many as odd because the expression Oh, how cute! sounds more natural to them. The use of oh for followed by an adjective isn't limited to cute, either. You can hear the interjections (oh) for cool!, for gross!, for fun!, for nice!, and for rude! as well.

These expressions are interesting because they are common not only in Utah but also in Minnesota.[1] What's more, they are ubiquitous in North Dakota.[2] What the heck? Although Minnesota and North Dakota border each other, they are geographically separated from Utah, and on the surface don't seem to have a lot in common. They are geographically separated, and on the surface they don't appear to be demographic cousins. However, the key to this mysterious connection may be their shared immigration patterns.

Graham[3] suggests that expressions beginning with oh for can be traced to Scandinavian languages. Figure 3.1 is taken from the 2000 US census. It shows the distribution of Americans who claim Danish origin; Utah, southeast Idaho, and a few counties in southern Minnesota are where the Danes settled in the greatest numbers. Could the for cute kind of interjections be due to the Danes?

The number of Iowa counties with large Danish-descended populations also stands out on this map. If the Danes are responsible for the oh for phrase, why isn't it mentioned as typical in Iowa? I did an informal scour of the internet and observed quite a few oh for + adjective expressions in posts related to Iowa. Perhaps no one in Iowa has taken note of it yet. If that's the case, we need to get a graduate student there to make it a topic of their dissertation.

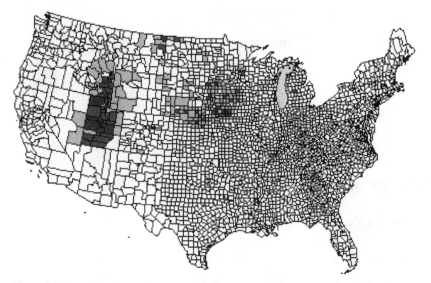

Figure 3.1. Counties with high concentrations of residents of Danish descent. (Credit: https://commons.wikimedia.org/wiki/File:Danish1346.gif)

On the other hand, maybe the Danish connection is all wrong. On the third hand, we need to remember that *oh for* may be attributed to Scandinavian influence generally, not just Danish influence. While North Dakota and Minnesota may not have a huge population of Danish descendants, those states contain a large number of Norwegian descendants (figure 3.2).

So, the question is how to connect those three states (and perhaps Iowa as well) with two different languages. It's important to know that people in Denmark, Norway, and Sweden can converse with each other without much difficulty. One Norwegian woman I spoke with confided that she often understood speakers from Sweden and Denmark better than she did the teenagers in her own country. We consider those languages to be different simply because they are spoken in distinct countries, but if history had taken a different turn and those languages had ended up housed in the same country, we'd call them dialects of the same language rather than distinct languages.

The Danes express the *for* + adjective phrase in their language with *hvor* followed by an adjective: *hvor sødt!* ("how cute!") and *hvor smukt!* ("how beautiful!"). At first glance, *hvor* doesn't look much like the English *for*, but the initial two letters in *hvor* are pronounced [v], making *hvor* a kissing cousin to English *for*. As these Danish immigrants acquired English, they transferred their

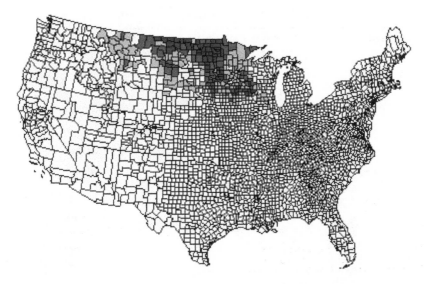

Figure 3.2. Counties with high concentrations of residents of Norwegian descent. (Credit: https://commons.wikimedia.org/wiki/File:Norwegian1346.gif)

interjections into the language and, because Danish *hvor* is English *for*, this resulted in expressions such as *for cute!* and *for beautiful!* This new construction could then spread from the Danish speakers to their English-speaking children and on to the rest of their neighbors, regardless of the neighbors' native language, and the expression was born.

We still need to tie North Dakota, Minnesota, and Norwegians to all of this, which is not tough to do. *For gross* and other similar expressions in Norwegian begin with the Norwegian word *for* followed by an adjective. So, the same expression in different parts of the United States had its genesis in two distinct, but closely related, languages.

Survey Results of *(Oh) For* + Adjective

Using the survey, I wanted to see how accepted the *oh for gross* kind of expression is, and if it's still alive. The survey participants were asked to rate the expressions *for cute* and *for cool* on how likely the participants were to use them as interjections in response to a particular scenario (table 3.1) They also rated the alternate expressions *that's cute/cool* and *how cute/cool*, but those expressions were included as distractor responses and weren't analyzed. The

Table 3.1. Test Questions and Responses for the *(Oh) For* + Adjective Interjections

Test Question	Test Responses

If you see an adorable little puppy, how likely are you say the following?	*How cute!*
	That's cute!
	For cute!
	  A Very likely +2
	  B Somewhat likely +1
	  C Somewhat unlikely −1
	  D Very unlikely −2

If you see something that you think is awesome, how likely are you to say the following?	*How cool!*
	That's cool!
	For cool!
	  A Very likely +2
	  B Somewhat likely +1
	  C Somewhat unlikely −1
	  D Very unlikely −2

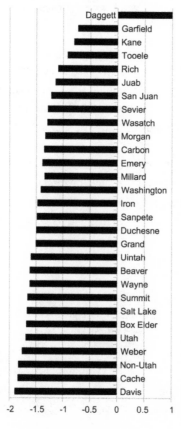

Figure 3.3. Mean rating to *(oh) for* + adjective expressions by county of residence.

scale the participants used in this task was coded numerically, but they did not see the associated numbers in the questionnaire.

The major finding is apparent in figure 3.3. With the exception of Daggett County, which garnered only eight responses, the means for the remaining counties were all negative, meaning that the vast majority of the participants indicated that they were not likely to use *for cute* or *for cool* in those contexts. One explanation for this result is that people just didn't see themselves using those expressions in the circumstances presented in the survey, but that if they saw other expressions in different scenarios they may have been more accepting of them. The other interpretation of the results is that the Utah Department of Self-Righteous Grammar Police has corrected or looked down on people for using *for* + adjective so much that people either don't want to admit that they use it or the police have effectively managed to squash its usage already. Another possibility is that older Utahns who may have used the phrase in the past have stopped as it fell out of use in the community.[4] This is one of those questions that can be answered only with further research.

In any event, the factors related to the participants' judgments appear in table 3.2. The sloping regression line in figure 3.4 indicates that younger people are less likely to accept the expression than older people are.

Gender also influenced the ratings; men rated the expressions much lower than women did (figure 3.5). Education was a significant factor as well, with the more educated ranking the expressions lower than those with less education did (figure 3.6).

Where the participants were raised was relevant (figure 3.7). Participants raised outside of the state gave a more negative rating to the expressions than Utahns raised inside and outside of the extended Wasatch Front did.[5] At the same time, Utahns raised in the extended Wasatch Front gave lower ratings than Utahns raised outside of the extended Wasatch Front, and people raised outside of the state rated the expressions lower than people raised on the Wasatch Front did.

It wasn't only where the participants were raised that was influential; it was also where they currently reside. There are differences between the three groups—those residing outside Utah, inside the limited Wasatch Front, and outside the limited Wasatch Front (figure 3.8). The post hoc analysis indicates that the ratings made by participants who were residing outside the limited Wasatch Front differ significantly from the other two groups.

Table 3.2. Statistical Results of the Judgments of *For* + Adjective Expressions

Predictor	F	Num df	Den df	p	R²
Age	25.90	1	1644	< .001	.016
Gender	19.68	1	1648	< .001	.017
Education	13.30	1	1670	< .001	.009
Region Raised In-Extended Wasatch	19.18	3	1646	< .001	.037
Region of Residence-Limited Wasatch	4.77	2	1636	0.009	.018

Marginal R^2 = .069
Conditional R^2 = .524

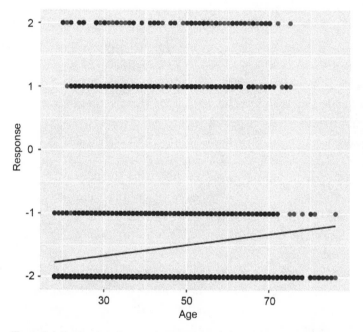

Figure 3.4. Scatterplot of age and responses to *(oh) for* + adjective expressions.

What can we take away from the survey results? First, the variables I've discussed, while significant, account for only 6.9 percent of the variance. It seems that a good chunk of the variance is explained by differences between test items and by differences between individual participants. Second, those who did not grow up in Utah were less likely to see themselves saying *for cool* or *for cute*. This finding points to the expression being a Utahism. Third, the fact that it was not well received by most participants but more accepted by older speakers indicates that the expression is dying out. Fourth, people who reside

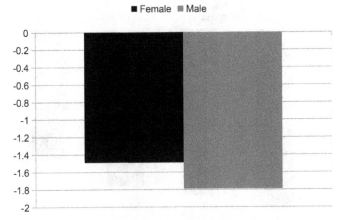

Figure 3.5. Mean ratings of *(oh) for* + adjective expressions by gender.

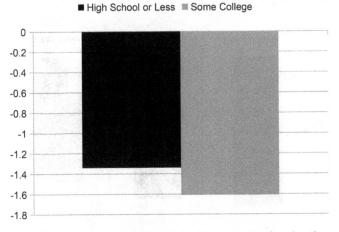

Figure 3.6. Mean ratings of *(oh) for* + adjective expressions by education.

outside of the state and those who live in the state's most populated areas rate the expression lower than people who reside in the state's less-populated areas do. These results, when coupled with the fact that the expression is less accepted by people with more education, suggest that expressions like *for cool* are associated more with rural areas and people who have less education. That combination may have given rise to the negative stigma that appears to be attached to the expression, which in turn may be partially responsible for its apparent decline.

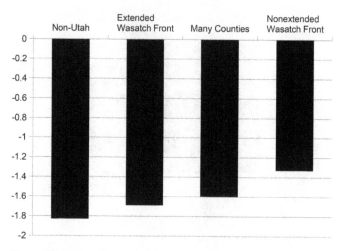

Figure 3.7. Mean ratings of *(oh) for* + adjective expressions by the region the participants were raised in.

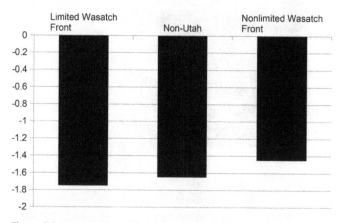

Figure 3.8. Mean ratings of *(oh) for* + adjective expressions by the participant's residence.

WE USED TO DO: PROPREDICATE *DO*

Is there anything about these sentences that bothers you?

    1a. At least I haven't heard the complaints that I used to do.
    2a. I think they could have done.
    3a. Do you want a hand, babe? I might do.

If you're like most Americans, you probably cringe at the *do* and *done* on the end and would prefer these instead:

1b. At least I haven't heard the complaints that I used to.
2b. I think they could have.
3b. Do you want a hand, babe? I might.

Most British English speakers, on the other hand, have no qualms about the *do* and *done*. In fact, the first three example sentences come from the British National Corpus.[6] Another instance of this grammatical structure is found in the lyrics of the song "Babe I'm Gonna Leave You," by the British rock band Led Zeppelin. Robert Plant croons: "I can hear it calling me the way it used to do."[7]

The use of the verb *do* in this way is called propredicate *do*. I'll refer to it as PPD. It is one of those quirks of English that the Brits use much more than the Yanks do, like how Americans convalesce *in the hospital* while the British do it *in hospital*. I'm not saying, however, that you'll never hear that kind of *do* in the United States.[8] For example, Hank Williams sang, "Why don't you love me the way you used to do?"[9]

In any case, PPD goes back a long way in English and can be found in the writings of Shakespeare[10] as well as in the speech of Harry Potter. It is abundantly attested in the English spoken in England.[11] Although you can find cases of PPD occurring before the twentieth century in England, the fact that you don't find many cases until the twentieth century[12] makes it look like PPD didn't catch on until then. The thing is, new variations in a language are first found in the spoken language, and by the time they show up in the written language it's usually safe to assume that the variations have been around in speech way before that point. As far as usage is concerned, in British English[13] PPD belongs to conversational speech and written fiction, but not to academic or journalistic writing.

Previous Studies on Propredicate *Do*

Interestingly, PPD has been studied in the speech of Utahns.[14] In her study, Di Paolo hypothesizes that PPD in Utah originated in the speech of English-immigrant members of the CJCLDS. These first European settlers arrived in Utah in 1847, and Di Paolo estimates that three years later, in 1850, some 88 percent of Utah foreign-born residents were English speakers who had their origins in British-governed populations, which included Canada. What's more, at that time, 15.4 percent of the Utah population consisted of foreign-born English speakers.

In 1850, the number of members of the CJCLDS in England outnumbered those in the United States, 30,747 to 26,911.[15] A large portion of those English members later migrated to Utah. Evans[16] estimates that at least 52,000 English people immigrated to the United States between 1837 and 1900. Another estimate puts that number at 100,000.[17] In any case, by 1877, half of the 140,000 people residing in what would become Utah were of British origin. This English influx is responsible for the fact that in 2000, 29 percent of Utahns claimed English ancestry, which is the largest percentage of any state in the country.[18]

Di Paolo[19] reported data from experiments in which three groups of people were asked how often they would use constructions with or without PPD. The following are two example questions:

1. I wonder if they made that book into a movie.
   (a) They may have made one.
   (b) They may have.
   (c) They may have done.
       1. most often
       2. sometimes
       3. least often or not at all
2. I don't believe Bill did his homework last night,
   (a) but he could have.
   (b) but he could have done.
   (c) but he could have done it.
   (d) but he coulda done.

In question 1, the study participants' task was to match the choices (a–c) with one of the three frequency responses. In question 2, they rated each of the four responses on a 1–7 scale that ranged from *always use it* to *never use it*.

The three groups that participated in the study were Utah members of the CJCLDS, members of the Fundamentalist Church of Jesus Christ of Latter-Day Saints (FLDS), and Utahns not belonging to either church. The FLDS participants in the study lived in Colorado City, Arizona, which is located just across the border from Utah. Early members of the FLDS Church separated from the

CJCLDS in the early twentieth century and established themselves in Hillsdale, Utah, and in Hillsdale's sister city, Colorado City, Arizona, which at the time was called Short Creek.

You may be wondering why the FLDS participants were included in Di Paolo's study. The idea was that their conservative culture and social isolation may have caused them to retain older dialectal characteristics of Utah. The general results of the study indicated that both the members of the CJCLDS and the FLDS church accepted the sentences containing PPD to a higher degree than Utahns who were members of neither church did. In other words, PPD may be an in-group religious marker.

Di Paolo's study was limited to the use of PPD after *may have* and *could have*, and it provides a snapshot of a point in time. In this section I want to build on Di Paolo's study by looking at the frequency of PPD in Utah across time by examining its appearance after a number of auxiliary verbs. I will then use those data to test the idea that PPD in Utah is attributable to the large English immigration. After that I will describe how I tested PPD in the dialect survey.

A Corpus Study of Propredicate *Do* in Utah

To study changes in the speech of Utahns across time, I needed a historical corpus. The best, and probably only, computer searchable corpus available is the LDS General Conference Corpus.[20] Twice a year, the CJCLDS holds a conference in which discourses are given, principally by church leaders. The corpus includes discourses and sermons from conferences held from 1851 to the present. It contains about 10,000 talks, which together consist of 25 million words.

I had my tireless research assistant, Jessica Brown, do the tedious job of searching the corpus for cases of PPD. One common place you find PPD is before a period, comma, or semicolon, which made Jessica's search for PPD fairly straightforward. For this reason, Jessica identified all cases of a number of highly frequent auxiliary verbs that preceded a period, comma, or semicolon. The auxiliaries considered were *ought to, have, used to, should, would, might, will, can,* and *may.* Jessica also found cases of these auxiliaries in the same context but followed by *do* or *done.* In this way it was possible to count not only instances of PPD, but also cases in which PPD was possible, but not used.

Of course, this search yielded many instances that were not relevant, which I had to remove by hand. For example, there are many cases of words such as *have, will, might,* and *can* that are not auxiliary verbs. When *have* means "possession,"

Table 3.3. Number of Instances of Propredicate *Do* Evaluated by the Speaker's Birth Date and Birthplace

Birth Date	Birthplace		
	Other	England	Utah
1797–1847	1,468	624	0
1848–1867	65	76	273
1868–1897	4	0	554
1898–1917	27	4	278
1918–1937	99	0	299
1938–1957	25	1	101

it's not an auxiliary. In the same way, when *will*, *might*, and *can* were used as nouns, rather than verbs, they were eliminated. People who give sermons often cite scripture or other sources, so these citations were removed as well.

Rather than organize the data according to the year in which the talk was given, I organized it by the speaker's birth year. Data from speakers born between 1797 and 1957 were included, but speakers born in non–English-speaking countries were removed from consideration. This work resulted in 3,898 instances in which PPD was possible. Of these, 887 contained PPD, and 3,011 were auxiliaries that were not followed by a form of *do* but that plausibly could be (e.g., *He could have done* versus *He could have*). These instances came from 338 different speakers, of whom only 23 were female. The distribution of cases by the speakers' place of birth and birth year is found in table 3.3.

Speakers from southeast Idaho were grouped with the Utah category because the characteristics of Utah English extend into southeast Idaho, which has close historical, religious, and dialectal ties with Utah. Speakers from England were kept separate from other countries in the UK and from Ireland, following Trudgill,[21] who argued that the use of PPD is a characteristic of the English language of England and not of the entire UK, nor of Ireland.

Results of the Corpus Study

I statistically analyzed the data to determine the effect of the speaker's date of birth and place of birth, as well as the auxiliary verb that was used. Table 3.4 indicates that birth year interacts with both auxiliary verb and place of birth. The interaction of auxiliary verb and birth year is illustrated in figure 3.9, where you can see that each verb follows a different trajectory over time. Figure 3.10

Table 3.4. Statistical Results of the Use of PPD in the Corpus

Predictors	χ^2	df	p
Birth Year	0.239	1	0.625
Birthplace	4.070	2	0.131
Auxiliary Verb	438.238	8	< .001
Auxiliary Verb by Birth Year	26.133	8	< .001
Birthplace by Birth Year	7.911	2	0.019

Marginal R^2: .305
Conditional R^2: .354

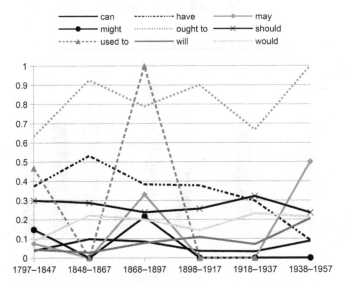

Figure 3.9. Proportion of propredicate *do*: Interaction of auxiliary verb and birth year.

shows which auxiliaries are most and least often found followed by a PPD. It would be tempting to assume that the frequency with which a verb is followed by a PPD is due to that verb's overall frequency, but a comparison of figures 3.10 and 3.11 dispels this notion. There is no correlation between the frequency of the verb in contemporary American English and its appearance in a PPD construction.[22] The frequency information was derived from the Corpus of Contemporary American English.[23] While total frequencies are reported for *ought to, used to, should,* and *would*, the frequencies of other words needed to be restricted to their use as auxiliaries. For this reason, the frequencies of

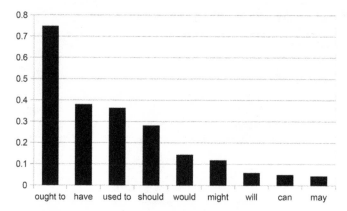

Figure 3.10. Proportion of use of PPD with each auxiliary verb.

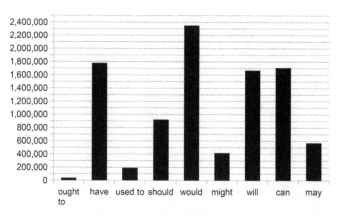

Figure 3.11. Frequency of each auxiliary in contemporary English.

might, *will*, *can*, and *may* were counted only when they were followed by verbs. The frequency of the auxiliary *have* was determined by counting how often it was followed by verbs ending in *-en* or *-ed*.

All this discussion of auxiliary verbs and frequencies isn't central to the point of this chapter, but when a tested variable is significant in the statistical analysis, someone may be interested, so I included it. What's more important is the relationship of the speaker's birth date and country of birth, which is illustrated in figure 3.12. In some cases, the lack of bars in the figure for some birth places is due to lack of instances. For example, in the data we collected there were no native-born Englishmen in a number of cohorts: Utahns born prior to 1847, born between 1868 and 1897, and born between 1918 and 1937.

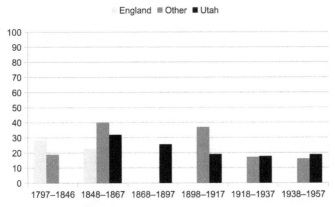

Figure 3.12. Percent of PPD by the speakers' year and place of birth.

The scarcity of instances from English-born speakers is evident in those born between 1898 and 1917, who provided only four cases of PPD or lack thereof, and English-born speakers born from 1938 to 1957, who accounted for only one instance. This paucity of data was motivation for excluding these years from the English-born speakers in figure 3.12 because the data would be highly unrepresentative. The same applies to speakers who were born between 1868 and 1897 and were from places other than Utah and England (i.e., from other places in the United States and from other countries), who contributed only four total cases. The raw data the table is based on appears in table 3.5.

Discussion of the Corpus Study

As I've mentioned, the variation in the use of PPD with different auxiliary verbs is difficult to interpret. It would be more interesting if the present-day frequencies could be compared to other more modern sources, either American or British English. At first glance, a study by Oger[24] looked promising for this purpose. Oger had extracted 486 cases of PPD from the British National Corpus,[25] which was compiled from the 1980s through the early 1990s, and had observed how frequently the construction appeared with various auxiliary verbs. From my perspective, the difficulty with her study is that it included only cases of PPD. Oger did not examine cases in which PPD was possible but not used (e.g., *Have you written the letter yet? No I haven't ___*). This omission makes it impossible to calculate how often PPD appears or does not appear in the context of the auxiliaries, which is why it is difficult to compare my study with Oger's.

Table 3.5. Percent of Propredicate *Do* by Speaker's Year of Birth and Place of Birth

			1797–1846	1848–1867	1868–1897	1898–1917	1918–1937	1938–1957
England	*Do*	Count	179	17		2		0
		% within Birth Year	28.70	22.40		50		0
	No *do*	Count	445	59		2		1
		% within Birth Year	71.30	77.60		50		100
Other	*Do*	Count	278	26	0	10	17	4
		% within Birth Year	18.90	40.00	0	37	17.20	16
	No *do*	Count	1190	39	4	17	82	21
		% within Birth Year	81.10	60.00	100	63	82.80	84
Utah	*Do*	Count		87	142	53	53	19
		% within Birth Year		31.90	25.60	19.10	17.70	18.80
	No *do*	Count		186	412	225	246	82
		% within Birth Year		68.10	74.40	80.90	82.30	81.20

Di Paolo's study[26] documents the use of PPD in Utah, and she ties PPD to religious groups in Utah. What she can't do is compare Utahns' use of PPD to other regions of the United States. It is entirely plausible that the use of PPD is prevalent elsewhere. Further research into the topic should use comparative data from Utah and other states, not only in contemporary speech but in historical speech as well. Nevertheless, the data from my study does indicate high rates of PPD usage outside of Utah. For example, for speakers born between 1918 and 1957 (figure 3.12) Utahns and speakers born in other places use PPD at quite similar rates. In the 1848–1867 and 1898–1917 cohorts, speakers who were neither English nor Utahns actually used PPD at much higher rates than the Utahns did.

Whenever I give people example sentences containing PPD and ask them who would talk like that, many people respond that PPD is something that they associate with older speakers. This response corresponds with the downward trend for Utah-born speakers seen in figure 3.12. This is good evidence that while the use of PPD may have been a prominent feature of Utah English, at least among the male leaders of the CJCLDS who were speaking in a formal setting, PPD is well on its way to extinction.

As already discussed, Utah received a much higher influx of English immigrants in the nineteenth and early twentieth centuries than other states did.

As a result, the population in Utah has the highest percentage of people with English heritage in the United States. This, coupled with the fact that PPD is much more prevalent in England than it is in the United States, leads one to conclude that PPD was introduced into Utah by the English immigrants who moved there. It is true that prior to the settlement of Utah, speeches given by English-born members of the CJCLDS contained a higher proportion of PPD use than did those given by speakers born outside of England. However, in the early Utah period (1848–1867) the use of PPD was much higher in the non-English-born groups.

What does this all mean? Well, there are a number of ways to interpret these findings. One is that this information is proof that the use of PPD had been adopted from the English-born speakers. If that were indeed the case, why would the non-English members born outside of Utah have adopted it and used it at higher levels than the Utah-born members? This is possibly because regardless of where they were born, the majority of those speakers lived in Utah or Idaho. For example, in 1860, 66 percent of CJCLDS members, regardless of their place of birth, lived in Utah. In 1880, 85 percent of church members lived in Utah and another 2.8 percent resided in neighboring Idaho.[27]

Accommodation is the phenomenon in which people adjust their speech so that they speak more like the people they are interacting with. The English speakers who moved to Utah came speaking many different dialects, and there was certainly a great deal of accommodation taking place in the state's early days, which eventually helped created a new dialect in Utah. In this early period of dialect contact, speakers who originally didn't use PPD may have adopted it from PPD users in the course of accommodation.

What doesn't quite fit into this theory is that the speakers born in England between 1848 and 1867 used PPD much less that those born in Utah or elsewhere. If these England-born people were the alleged instigators of PPD in Utah, you'd expect their usage to be equal to or higher than that of the other groups. Of course, the argument could also be made that the English, who were surrounded by speakers for whom PPD was not customary, could have adjusted their speech in the direction of the majority. However, that reasoning is a bit contradictory. It would involve non–English-born people adopting a PPD from the English, while at the same time the English were accommodating their speech to a variety that did not use PPD. A third possibility is that the English immigrants introduced PPD and it caught on for a short period of time but soon began its slow decline in the speech of Utahns.

To make matters even harder to disentangle, Butters[28] shows that PPD in England was not common until after World War I. In like manner, Joos[29] places its rise in the twentieth century. If this is the case, PPD would not have been common in the speech of the England-born immigrants from the nineteenth century. How then could it be attributed to them in that century? There are two ways to look at this question. The first is that PPD wasn't taken to Utah by the nineteenth-century English immigrants, but instead by the English settlers who immigrated in the early part of the twentieth century. However, if that were true we'd expect to see a spike in its usage after the 1920s, but there is none. Instead, PPD use shows a steady decline in the speech of Utahns born between 1867 and 1937. The small increase in the 1938–1957 cohort doesn't appear to be particularly different from the 1918–1937 group.

The second way to consider the question is to understand that the sources showing that the use of PPD doesn't become popular until after World War I are written documents. It is very plausible that PPD was actually quite common in speech but didn't make it into more formal writing until after World War I. This is another way to interpret the data in figure 3.12.

Concerning religion's influence on the use of PPD, Di Paolo[30] shows that members of the CJCLDS and FLDS are more accepting of PPD, something the corpus study can't address. As I already noted, Di Paolo also assumes that PPD is used more often in Utah than in other states, yet we have no comparative data to confirm that hunch. In contrast, the data from my corpus study show higher use of PPD by those born outside of Utah and England in 1848–1867 and 1898–1917. Very similar rates were found for those born between 1918 and 1957. All of this data suggest that in terms of PPD usage Utahns may not be outliers in the United States. It is possible that PPD use in Utah varied widely depending on the speaker's gender or on the speech's degree of formality. The corpus data I've presented primarily reflects the speech of older men speaking in a highly formal setting. The rates of PPD usage may diverge greatly when speech from other speakers, spoken in other contexts, is considered. Clearly, more historical and contemporary sociolinguistic studies are warranted to answer these questions more precisely.

Survey Investigation of Propredicate *Do*

The studies I discussed in the previous section show that the use of PPD is related to religion and that PPD is being used less and less over time. To better

Table 3.6. Test Questions and Responses for Propredicate *Do.*

Test Question	Test Words and Responses

Suppose that you feel you should exercise more, and someone asks you "Do you exercise regularly?" how likely are you to give these responses to that question?	A *I ought to exercise*
	B *I ought to*
	C *I ought to do*
	  Very likely +2
	  Somewhat likely +1
	  Somewhat unlikely −1
	  Very unlikely −2

If you skied when you were younger and someone asks you "Do you ski?" how likely are you to give these responses to that question?	A *I used to*
	B *I used to do*
	C *I used to ski*
	  Very likely +2
	  Somewhat likely +1
	  Somewhat unlikely −1
	  Very unlikely −2

If you have plans for Friday and someone asks you "Can you babysit on Friday?" how likely are you to give these responses to that question?	A *I would babysit, but I'm busy*
	B *I would, but I'm busy*
	C *I would do, but I'm busy*
	  Very likely +2
	  Somewhat likely +1
	  Somewhat unlikely −1
	  Very unlikely −2

Your friend is a contestant on a game show and you felt he would win. After the show is over another friend asks you "Did you hear that Jake won the grand prize on the game show?" How likely are you to give these responses to that question?	A *I predicted he would win before it started*
	B *I predicted he would do before it started*
	C *I predicted he would before it started*
	  Very likely +2
	  Somewhat likely +1
	  Somewhat unlikely −1
	  Very unlikely −2

understand these conclusions, I included eight test items with PPD in my survey (table 3.6). Each participant saw only four of the eight items. The numeric values of each response were not seen by the participants, and only the responses containing PPD were analyzed.

The first result that stands out is that the average response was -1.6, or in other words, between *somewhat unlikely* and *very unlikely*. The average answer to each of the eight test items ranged from -1.13 to -1.84, meaning that the

Table 3.6. Test Questions and Responses for Propredicate *Do. (continued)*

Test Question	Test Words and Responses
You are learning to play the piano but are having a hard time practicing. A friend says this to you: "I told you to practice the piano every day or you'll never be able to play well." How likely are you to respond to their statement in the following ways?	A *I know I should have done. I'll do better next week.* B *I know I should have. I'll do better next week.* C *I know I should have practiced. I'll do better next week.* Very likely +2 Somewhat likely +1 Somewhat unlikely −1 Very unlikely −2
You are contemplating putting lots of money into an investment. However, your spouse is hesitant. In order to convince them it's a good idea, how likely are you to say the following sentences?	A *If it requires our entire life savings, as it may require, it's worth the chance to earn a small fortune.* B *If it requires our entire life savings, as it may do, it's worth the chance to earn a small fortune.* C *If it requires our entire life savings, as it may, it's worth the chance to earn a small fortune.* Very likely +2 Somewhat likely +1 Somewhat unlikely −1 Very unlikely −2
You and your sister are waiting for the results of a DNA test that you both took to see if you have the same father. How likely would you be to say the following sentences?	A *When the results arrive, which they will do at some point, then we will finally know the truth.* B *When the results arrive, which they will at some point, then we will finally know the truth.* C *When the results arrive, which they will arrive at somepoint, then we will finally know the truth.* Very likely +2 Somewhat likely +1 Somewhat unlikely −1 Very unlikely −2
You are an arrogant artist. While discussing how fantastic your art is to a reporter, how likely are you to say the following sentences?	A *I created what no one else could do.* B *I created what no one else could.* C *I created what no one else could create.* Very likely +2 Somewhat likely +1 Somewhat unlikely −1 Very unlikely −2

Table 3.7. Statistical Results of the Ratings to Test Responses Containing Propredicate *Do*

Predictor	F	Num. df	Den. df	p	R²
Region Raised in—Extended Wasatch Front	7.500	3	1631	< .002	—
Age	12.161	1	1638	< .001	.005
Percent of Life in Utah	.2531	1	1654	.627	—
Gender	.146	1	1619	.702	—
Education	11.896	1	1683	< .001	.003
Religion	.757	2	1658	.469	—
Region Raised in by Gender	3.333	3	1642	.019	.009
Percent of Life in Utah by Religion	4.720	2	1680	.009	.005

Marginal R^2 = .017
Conditional R^2 = .285

participants generally didn't see themselves responding with PPD to any of the test items. Lillie's survey[31] corroborated this as well. It contained one question that included PPD (i.e., *She must ___, have done/have*) and only 4 percent of the respondents chose *have done*. The factors that influenced the ratings in my survey appear in table 3.7.

Although the county the participant was raised in was not significant by itself, I include those data here because it is probably of interest to many readers (figure 3.13; counties preceded by an asterisk had fewer than ten responses). The interaction between region and gender, on the other hand, was significant and is illustrated in figure 3.14. The post hoc analysis shows that the differences between the region by gender groups center on the males who were raised outside of the extended Wasatch Front. They comprise the group that had less-negative views of PPD. They were more accepting of PPD when compared with the females in their region, with the females and males from the extended Wasatch Front, with the females not raised in the state, and with the females raised in many counties. Females not raised in the extended Wasatch Front differed from Wasatch Front males, and from males not raised in Utah. In general, these results support the finding from Lillie's survey that those from rural areas chose the response that used PPD more than those from urban areas did.

The effect of participants' age is illustrated in figure 3.15, in which the up-sloping regression line indicates that, in comparison to older participants, younger participants were much less likely to see themselves using PPD; this finding is similar to Lillie's.[32] As far as educational level is concerned, the more

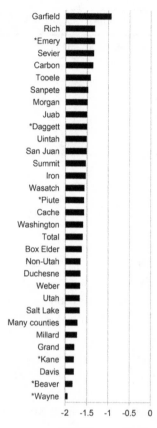

Figure 3.13. Ratings of propredicate *do* by county raised in.

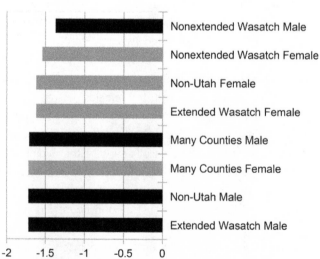

Figure 3.14. Ratings of propredicate *do* by region raised in and gender.

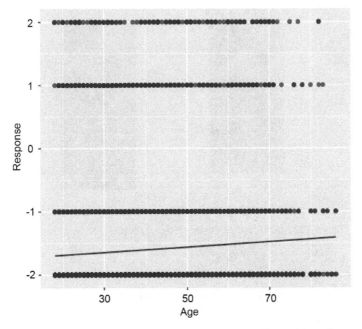

Figure 3.15. Scatterplot of ages and responses to propredicate *do* questions.

educated participants gave lower ratings to sentences containing PPD than did the less educated participants (figure 3.16).

In her study, Di Paolo[33] found significant differences in her participants' ratings depending on the participants' religion, something that is borne out in this survey as well (figure 3.17). While the practicing members of the CJCLDS gave less negative ratings than those who had lived longer in the state did, the ratings given by members of other denominations became more negative the more time the respondents had spent in the state. No trend is apparent for nonpracticing CJCLDS members.

Although the acceptance of phrases containing PPD is quite low overall, the differences between religious groups could be interpreted to show that PPD is an in-group characteristic. Practicing members of the CJCLDS may cue into the use of PPD over time, while members of other religions who have spent a good proportion of their lives in Utah appear to rate PPD more unfavorably, possibly because they perceive it as a feature of the group they do not belong to. Perhaps the lack of effect over time for nonpracticing members

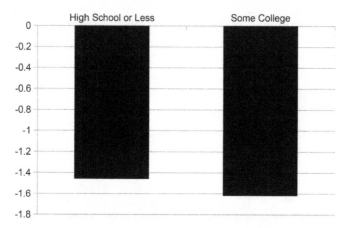

Figure 3.16. Mean responses to propredicate *do* questions by education.

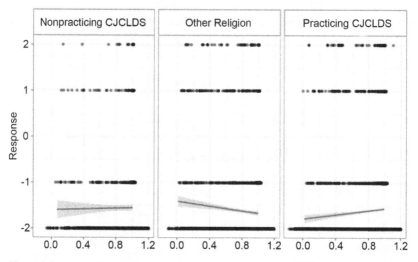

Figure 3.17. Scatterplot of ratings of propredicate *do* questions and the proportion of the participant's life spent in Utah by religion.

of the CJCLDS represents this group's intermediate state between the other religious groups.

The variables I've discussed in this section are significantly related to the ratings of PPD. However, they account for only 1.7 percent of what is going on, which means that there are many other important factors that govern the rating of PPD besides the ones presented here. Nevertheless, when the variables we've discussed are considered together, they point to the use of PPD as an older feature of Utah English; PPD is more accepted by practicing members of the CJCLDS who have spent a greater proportion of their life in the state, as well as by older speakers and by males who were raised in more rural areas. In a similar vein, PPD is less accepted by the more educated. The corpus data indicate that the use of PPD has been declining in Utah since the nineteenth century, which is something that the age differences in the survey also attest to. When these factors are considered along with the fact that most of the survey responses were either *somewhat unlikely* or *very unlikely*, they strongly suggest that the PPD construction may have been a prominent feature of Utah English in the past but that it is quickly winding down to extinction in the state.

4

Pop or Soda?

Individual Words and Pronunciations in Utah

CREEK

Phonetic symbols used in this section

[i] as in l**ea**p
[ɪ] as in l**i**p
[ɛ] as in sl**e**pt

I've heard people say that a sure way to tell if someone is from Utah is if they pronounce *creek* as *cr[ɪ]ck*. If that were true, then Tom Sawyer would have been a Utahn. Mark Twain put these words in his character's Missouri mouth: "Just as I was passing a place where a kind of a cowpath crossed the crick, here comes a couple of men tearing up the path as tight as they could foot it."[1] I hate to break it to those people, but that particular pronunciation was actually found all across the United States in one dialect survey.[2]

I'm sure there are language purists who insist that the proper pronunciation has to be *cr[i]ck* because the double *ee* spelling in English gives us *feet, sweet,* and *keep* with the vowel [i], which no one would pronounce with the vowel [ɪ] as if they were *fit, swit,* or *kip*. Unfortunately, the English spelling system is notoriously inexact, which makes appeals to spelling like these quite shaky. I'll simply cite the word *been*, which no American who wasn't trying on a British accent for effect, would ever pronounce in the same way as *bean. Been* is normally rendered as *bin* b[ɪ]n or *Ben* b[ɛ]n in the United States, and in like manner *creek* can be either *cr[ɪ]ck* or *cr[i]ck*.

What may add to the purists' horror is that even the esteemed Merriam Webster dictionary can't help but cite *cr[ɪ]ck* as a pronunciation of *creek*.[3] Dictionary compilers simply document what they hear the speakers of the language say. They don't invent words or pronunciations to grace the pages

68

of their volumes and then insist that those words or pronunciations be used by English speakers. The written words in the dictionary have always been based on the spoken words, not vice-versa. I trust it is clear that cr[ɪ]ck, while common in Utah, is common elsewhere as well, which disqualifies it from being an exclusively Utah term.

Survey Results for *Creek*

The pronunciation of *creek* in Utah has drawn attention for quite a while. Pardoe discussed it in 1935,[4] and in Lillie's 1997 study,[5] she observed that 31.4 percent of her participants said cr[ɪ]ck and 61.1 percent cr[i]ck. The cr[ɪ]ck pronunciation was more common in the older respondents and in those who lived in the central part of the state, followed by people who lived in the southern portion. That pronunciation was least frequent in the north.

People taking my survey were shown one of the questions in table 4.1 and asked to match the vowel in *creek* to the vowel in one of two response words. The results were about half and half, 793 [ɪ] and 806 [i]. You'd expect the proportion of [i] answers to be similar for both of the test words *crease* and *creep*. In the same way, you'd expect *Chris* and *Krip* to be assigned similar vowels as well. Instead, the results were the unexpected ones shown in figure 4.1. What may have thrown people off was the word *Krip*, which was my misspelling of *Crip*, the LA street gang, a term which may not have been familiar to many of the participants anyway. I threw out the responses with *Krip* and analyzed only the responses that matched either *crease* or *creep*. No variable came close to being significant. In my gut I think that there is some interesting variation in the pronunciation of *creek* in Utah and I trust that some budding linguist will take up this issue in the future and find out what it is.

Table 4.1. Test Question and Responses for *Creek*

Test Question	Test Words and Responses
How do you pronounce the highlighted part of the word ___? Like the word ___.	**cree**k A **crea**se B **Chri**s **cree**k A **Kri**p B **cree**p

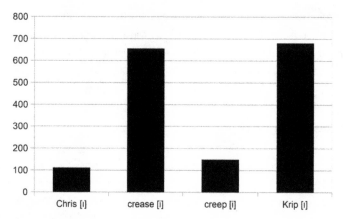

Figure 4.1. Number of responses to the words that the participants perceived to have the same vowel as *creek*.

ROOF

Phonetic symbols used in this section

[ʊ] as in b**oo**k
[u] as in s**ue**d
[o] as in l**oa**d

For many people, *roof* rhymes with *proof*; both words have the vowel sound [u]. Some people claim that only Utahns fail to rhyme *roof* and *proof* and instead give *roof* the same vowel sound as *would*: [ʊ]. The evidence for the correct pronunciation, they claim, is in the spelling: *oo* says [u]. This pronunciation is evident in a myriad of words such as *spoof, aloof, food, choose, moon, shoot, google, mood,* and so on.

I don't dispute that those words have [u] as their vowel; I merely point out the messiness of English spelling that sometimes puts seemingly random letters in words that no one in their right mind would ever pronounce. Consider the *s* in *island*, the *w* in *sword*, the *t* in *castle*, and the *gh* in *fight, caught,* and *though,* to mention a few. Evidence from English spelling is so fluffy that it would certainly never hold up in a court of law. The truth is that in English most letters have several pronunciations. Take the letter *a*, for instance. It rolls off the tongue in a different way in *last, taste, large,* and *allow.* The same is true for *oo*. It is a written representation of the [u] vowel in *proof* and *moon*, but it is used to represent the [o] sound as well, as in *floor* and *door*. Even more confusing, *oo* is also used to write the [ʊ] sound in words such as *good*, *took*, *hook*, *brook*, *soot*, *foot*, and *book*. The moral of the story is that spelling is poor evidence of a word's "true" pronunciation.

In fact, there are a few words spelled with *oo* whose pronunciation varies from speaker to speaker. The words *broom*, *room*, *hoof*, and *root* are among them, along with *roof*. It's actually next to impossible to find a dividing line on a map denoting where in the country *roof* is pronounced *r[u]f* and where it's pronounced *r[ʊ]f*. The results of one dialect survey[6] show both pronunciations in Utah as well as in many different parts of the country. In a more recent survey,[7] *r[ʊ]f* was seen to be well established in the Midwest. One takeaway from this fact is that you shouldn't look to *roof* when you're trying to find a unique Utah pronunciation. The other is that perhaps Utah got this pronunciation from the Midwest. In the nineteenth century, members of the CJCLDS spent a great deal of time in Illinois, Missouri, and Ohio before fleeing to the Rocky Mountains. As they left the Midwest, they may have packed *r[ʊ]f* in their wagons and handcarts alongside their other supplies.

Survey Results for *Roof*

The remaining question is how the distinct pronunciations of *roof* are distributed in Utah. My survey presented each participant with one of the test words in table 4.2. The participants matched *roof* to the responses with [u] in 80 percent of the cases and to [ʊ] in only 20 percent, which demonstrates that [ʊ] is not the most common pronunciation of the word in the state. Significant predictors for this result were the participants' age and the interaction of the age with the region the participants were raised in (table 4.3).[8] Please note the extremely

Table 4.2. Test Question and Responses for *Roof*

Test Question	Test Words and Responses
How do you pronounce the highlighted part of the word ___? Like the word ___.	r**oo**f
	A p**u**t
	B p**oo**t
	r**oo**f
	A k**oo**k
	B c**oo**k

Table 4.3. Statistical Results of the Pronunciation of *Roof*

Predictor	χ^2	df	p	R^2
Age	3.31	1	.069	
Region Raised in—Limited Wasatch Front	12.63	2	.006	
Age by Region Raised in	9.51	3	.023	.027

McFadden's R^2 = .027

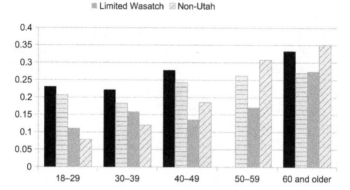

Figure 4.2. Effect of age by region raised in on the pronunciation of *roof* as r[ʊ]f.

small R^2 value, which tells us that these predictor variables account for only a small part of the variance here. With that in mind, it is clear in figure 4.2 that older speakers are more likely to say r[ʊ]f than younger speakers are. This may indicate that r[ʊ]f is a dying pronunciation in the state. With the exception of the oldest speakers, those who were raised outside of the limited Wasatch Front preferred r[ʊ]f more than participants who were raised in the limited Wasatch Front.

POP, SODA, OR COKE

Imagine that your friend asks you if you want a Coke and you respond, "Sure, give me a Pepsi." If your friend doesn't bat an eye and hands you a Pepsi, what part of the country are you in? You'd have to be in the South, where carbonated drinks, regardless of the label on the can, are all called Coke. As the map in figure 4.3 shows, apart from the South, the rest of the country calls carbonated

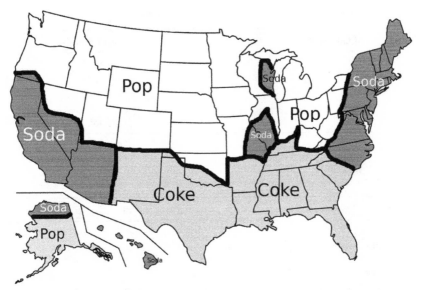

Figure 4.3. The word for carbonated drink by region. (Credit: Original unmodified blank map of U.S. created by Kaboom88, public domain, https://commons.wikimedia.org/w/index .php?curid=2989307)

beverages either *soda* or *pop*.[9] Utah falls squarely in the *pop* region according to this map, so you may assume that there's nothing interesting going on there. The trouble with drawing lines on a map is that they don't show the actual shades of gray that exist, not only spatially but also socially.

In one study the two most common words used were *soda* (45 percent) and *pop* (34 percent).[10] Lillie[11] asked Utahns what they called carbonated beverages, and unsurprisingly, *pop* was most common followed by *soda*, *Coke*, and *soft drink* (47.2 percent, 22.8 percent, 9.8 percent, and 2.6 percent, respectively). She noticed that older speakers preferred *pop* more than younger speakers did and that the use of *soda* increased with the level of education. Geographically, *Coke* was more common in the southern part of the state, while *soda* was the more popular term in the northern and central counties.

The question the participants answered in my survey appears in table 4.4. The outcome appears in figure 4.4. Analyzing the data was tricky because the participants chose between five options, not just two, so I performed three logistic regressions. One contrasted *soda* and all other responses combined, another contrasted *pop* and all other responses combined, and the third

Table 4.4. Test Question and Responses for Carbonated Drink

Test Question	Test Responses
What is your general term for carbonated drinks?	A *pop*
	B *Coke*
	C *soda*
	D *soda pop*
	E *soft drink*

Table 4.5. Statistical Results of *Soda* versus All Other Responses

Predictor	χ^2	df	p	R^2
Age	115.05	1	< .001	.070
Percent of Life in Utah	6.03	1	0.014	.004
Education	6.59	1	0.010	9.84e−4
Population of County Raised In	30.54	1	< .001	.038
Region of Residence—Limited Wasatch Front	13.55	2	0.001	.022
Religion	28.08	3	< .001	.016

McFadden's R^2 = .145

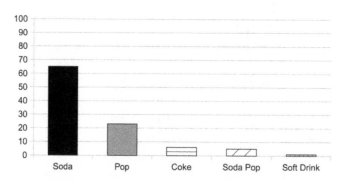

Figure 4.4. Percent of responses for carbonated drink.

contrasted *pop/soda* against all other responses. The results of the *soda* vs. all others regression are summarized in table 4.5.

    Soda is the most common term used in the state to refer to carbonated beverages. This is especially true among younger Utahns, where there is a definite age-apparent shift away from all other terms for carbonated drink

■ Soda ■ Pop ⊟ Coke ⊠ Soda Pop ⊞ Soft Drink

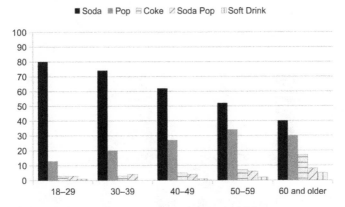

Figure 4.5. Percent of responses for carbonated drink by age.

■ Soda ■ Pop ⊟ Coke ⊠ Soda Pop ⊞ Soft Drink

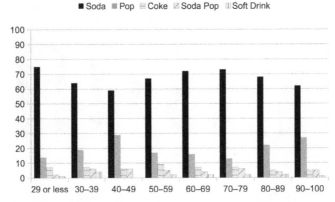

Figure 4.6. Percent of responses for carbonated drink by the percent of life spent in Utah.

(figure 4.5). While age has a linear relationship to the use of *soda*, the same thing is not true for the effect of the percent of a participant's life spent in Utah (figure 4.6). This is partially because the actual percent for each participant was included in the model, while the graph distorts that a bit by breaking the continuous percent into eight discrete categories. However, the data are so far from linear that the coefficients aren't very representative of the actual trends. The preference for *soda* has two peaks, one among speakers who have spent the least amount of their lives in Utah, and another among those who have spent about 60–79 percent of their lives in Utah. This may indicate an interesting trend that needs to be investigated more thoroughly.

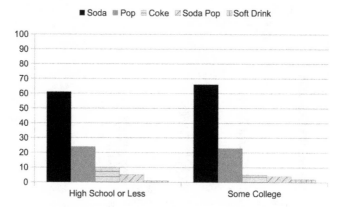

Figure 4.7. Terms for carbonated drink by education.

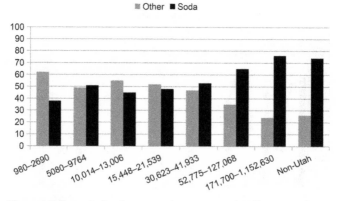

Figure 4.8. Percent of *soda* versus other responses by the population of the county the participant was raised in.

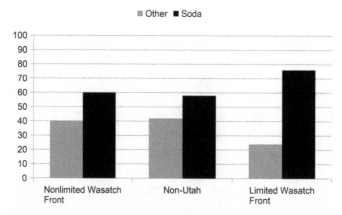

Figure 4.9. Percent of *soda* versus other responses by participant's region of residence.

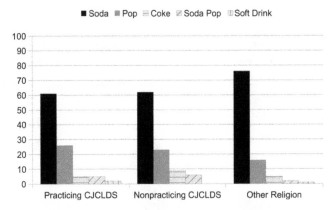

Figure 4.10. Percent of responses to carbonated drink by religion.

Education also plays a small role in the participants' responses to this question (figure 4.7). Participants with more education preferred *soda* slightly more than the other respondents did, while the use of *Coke* drops with further education. Some of the regional variation in the state is based on the population of the county that each participant was raised in (figure 4.8), as well as the participant's region of residence (figure 4.9). *Soda* is preferred more by people raised in the more populated areas of Utah. It also dominates in speakers who reside in the limited Wasatch Front when compared with those residing outside of the limited Wasatch Front and Utahns not currently living in the state.

The influence of religion on English in Utah has been observed in other linguistic studies,[12] and that influence is borne out in this study as well. Members of the CJCLDS, both practicing and nonpracticing, preferred *soda* to a smaller degree than those who have other religious preferences (figure 4.10).

In the second analysis, *pop* was pitted against all other words for carbonated beverages (table 4.6). Only 23 percent of the responses were for *pop*. The results largely reverse-mirrored those of *soda*. The preference for *pop* increases with age (figure 4.11), and the relationship between age and the percent of one's life spent in Utah is not linear (figure 4.12). *Pop* was preferred more often by people from counties with small populations (figure 4.13) and by those living outside of the limited Wasatch Front and outside of the state (figure 4.14). Practicing members of the CJCLDS preferred *pop* more than those of other faiths (figure 4.15).

Table 4.6. Statistical Results of *Pop* versus All Other Responses

Predictor	χ^2	df	*p*	R^2
Age	30.9	1	<.001	.022
Percent of Life in Utah	17.1	1	<.001	.008
Population of County Raised In	43.7	1	<.001	.055
Region of Residence-Limited Wasatch Front	24.9	2	<.001	.032
Religion	20.0	3	<.001	.013

McFadden's R^2 = .117

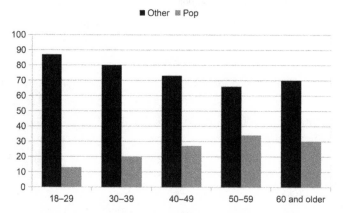

Figure 4.11. Percent of *pop* responses by age.

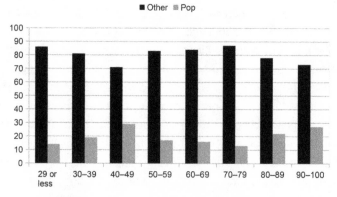

Figure 4.12. Percent of *pop* responses by the percent of life spent in Utah.

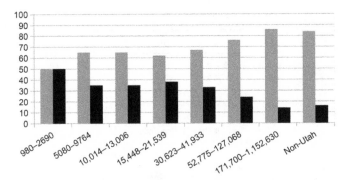

Figure 4.13. Percent of *pop* responses by the population of county the participants were raised in.

Other ■ Pop

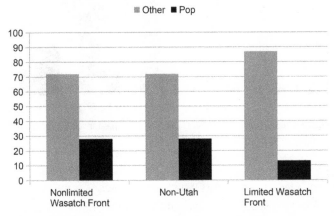

Figure 4.14. Percent of *pop* responses by the participants' region of residence.

■ Other ■ Pop

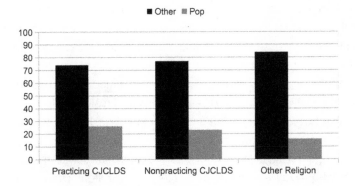

Figure 4.15. Percent of responses to *pop* by religion.

Table 4.7. Results of the Statistical Analysis of *Coke/soda pop/soft drink* against *soda/pop*

Predictor	χ^2	df	p	R^2
Age	87.50	1	< .001	.074
Education	4.24	1	0.039	.002

McFadden's R^2 = .078

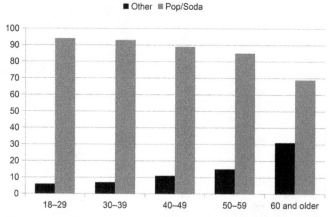

Figure 4.16. Percent of *coke/soda pop/soft drink* responses compared to *soda/pop* responses by age.

The final analysis pitted the least common responses (i.e., *soda pop, Coke,* and *soft drink*) against *pop* and *soda* combined (table 4.7). It was principally the oldest participants who preferred a term other than *soda* or *pop* to refer to carbonated drinks (figure 4.16). The more educated respondents were slightly less likely to prefer *soda pop, Coke,* or *soft drink* over *soda/pop* (figure 4.17).

Utah is usually categorized as a *pop* area, along with most of the states in the central northern part of the country. In 1997, Lillie[13] registered *pop* as the most frequent term in Utah, but she also observed that *soda* was catching on among the younger respondents. The apparent-time shift she documented twenty-three years ago has now been verified as a real-time shift away from *pop.* Utah is now a *soda* state, but *pop* is the older term. It is preferred more by those who were raised in or reside in the more rural parts of the state, by those who have spent a larger percent of their life in the state (with the exception of those who have lived around 40 percent of their life in Utah), by the less educated, and by members of the CJCLDS. This state of affairs is most likely

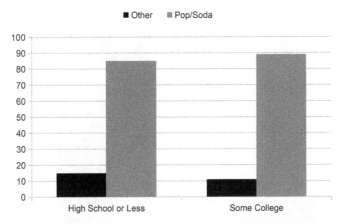

Figure 4.17. Percent of *coke/soda pop/soft drink* responses compared to *soda/pop* responses by education.

the result of urbanization and the influx of out-of-staters, especially to the Wasatch Front region.

HURRICANE

Phonetic symbols used in this section

[eɪ] as in p**ai**n
[ə] as in **a**bove
[æ] as in m**a**n
[ɨ] as in bus**e**s
[ɑ] as in f**a**ther

Given the desert climate and landlocked location of the town of Hurricane in Utah's southern region, one wonders how it got its name to begin with. According to town history, in 1896 a gust of wind caught Erastus Snow by surprise when it blew the top off of his buggy. The force of the gust was so hurricane-like to Erastus that he christened the nearby prominent point Hurricane Hill, after which the town was subsequently named.[14]

Another intriguing question is why the residents of the town pronounce Hurricane *Hurric[ə]n* rather than the more common *Hurric[eɪ]n*. The unique pronunciation of the town name serves to distinguish who is local and who's an outsider. That kind of linguistic group marking is actually quite a common phenomenon. New Yorkers, for example, are more likely to pronounce *Manhattan* as M[ə]nhattan rather than M[æ]nhattan. In like manner, residents of Prescott, Arizona, call their hometown Presc[ɨ]tt, not Presc[ɑ]tt. In Utah, outsiders who are aware of how native Hurricanites refer to their town have been known to snicker at the unusual pronunciation. It is interesting, however, that the residents' supposedly idiosyncratic, novel, or, heaven forbid, corrupted pronunciation is actually not unique at all.

The Cambridge Dictionary[15] lists both an American and British version of *hurricane*. The American pronunciation is *hurric[eɪ]n*, while the British pronunciation is *hurric[ə]n*, so the question isn't why the pronunciation was altered in southern Utah; the question is how a Britishism made its way into the Utah desert. Now, most of the early settlers of Hurricane came from other parts of Utah,[16] so that information isn't very telling. However, Utah in general was swamped with immigrants from Britain, who made Utah the state with the highest concentration of British ancestry in the country.[17] Those immigrants didn't simply drop off their speech patterns at Ellis Island; they brought their old-world pronunciations, along with their genetic material, to the Beehive State. *Hurricane* may have been one of the terms they passed onto Utahns, where it appears to have stuck only in the pronunciation of this town.

TOUR

Phonetic symbols used in this section

[u] as in l**ew**d
[ʊə] as in British s**ewe**r (where the *r* isn't pronounced)
[aʊ] as in s**ou**r
[o] as in l**oa**d

When I was a high school student, I was told that my pronunciation of *tour*, the one that rhymes with *core*, was very typical for a Utahn. That puzzled me because I knew words spelled with *o-u-r* like *four* and *pour* that no one in their right mind would pronounce f[u]r or p[u]r. Plus, Seymour the Cat was definitely called Seym[o]r, not Seym[u]r. Of course, I've already pointed out that

English spelling is not a great source of evidence for precise pronunciations because *o-u* also gives [aʊ] in *hour* and *sour*. In spite of all this, when I moved out of state I folded to my linguistic insecurity and consciously changed my pronunciation to *t[u]r*.

But, you are asking, that is the common pronunciation in Utah, right? Well, in Lillie's survey[18] it was about half and half: 54.9 percent *t[u]r* and 44.9 percent *t[o]r*. Now, there are a good number of people who are pretty convinced that there's something wrong with *t[o]r*—that pronunciation raises lots of eyebrows in internet discussion groups—but it's not just about its use in Utah. When I searched the internet, I found the pronunciation mentioned in the speech of people from New Jersey, Ohio, California, New York, the East Coast, and Canada, which leads me to be fairly confident that it's not unique to Utah.

The Cambridge Dictionary[19] cites *t[u]r* as the American pronunciation and *t[ʊə]r* as British. This is similar to the entry in the Oxford Learners Dictionaries,[20] except that this dictionary gives it a second British pronunciation, *t[o]r*, where the final *r* is optional, of course. As I've discussed in previous sections, Utah became the home of many British people, and that makes me suspicious that these immigrants may have introduced or solidified *t[o]r* in the state.

Survey Results for *Tour*

In the survey, participants were asked only one question about the pronunciation of *tour* (table 4.8). *T[o]r* was chosen by 52 percent and *t[u]r* by 48 percent. Table 4.9 shows the predictors that were significantly related to the result. More *t[o]r* pronunciations were found in participants who have spent a higher percent of their life in the state (figure 4.18). This may place *t[o]r* as the prestige pronunciation in the state. In 1997, Lillie[21] observed an age difference in which the eighteen- to thirty-year-olds pronounced the word as *t[o]r* 59.8 percent of the time and speakers fifty-five and older did so at a lower rate of 46.8 percent. That apparent-time difference may have pointed to a shift in which *t[o]r* was on its way to dominating *t[u]r* in the state. Instead, twenty-three years later

Table 4.8. Test Question and Responses for the Pronunciation of *Tour*

Test Question	Test Responses
How do you pronounce the highlighted part of the word **tou**r? Like the word ___.	A **too**t
	B **to**te

Table 4.9. Statistical Results for the Pronunciation of *Tour*

Predictor	χ^2	df	*p*	R^2
Percent of Life in Utah	11.0	1	< .001	.044
Age	18.4	1	< .001	.009
Region Raised in—3 Regions	22.9	3	< .001	.048
Religion	11.3	3	0.010	.007

McFadden's R^2 = .067

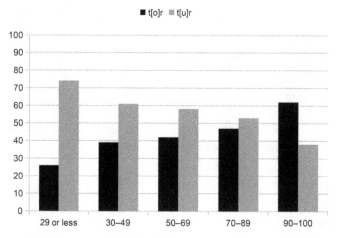

Figure 4.18. Percent of pronunciation responses to *tour* by percent of life spent in Utah.

we find a similar distribution. Younger Utahns still prefer *t[o]r*. Only about 43 percent of Utahns fifty and older prefer *t[o]r*, while that number increases to 56 percent for those between eighteen and forty-nine. That is, *t[o]r* really hasn't gained any ground, as the age difference in 1997 would have predicted. However, we do see a higher preference for *t[o]r* in younger speakers (figure 4.19).

The region the participants were raised in, as well as the religion they belong to, played a part in their pronunciation of *tour*. As you can see in figure 4.20, those raised outside of Utah preferred *t[u]r* much more than those raised within the state. The post hoc statistics bear out this result as well. Central Utah differs from all of the regions, while the small difference between southern and northern Utah is not significant. Put in other terms, *t[o]r* is definitely less common among those not raised in the state, while within the state it is somewhat more of a central Utah feature.

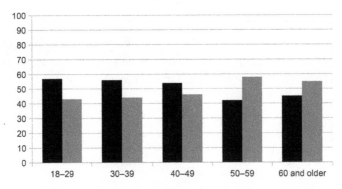

Figure 4.19. Percent of pronunciation responses to *tour* by age.

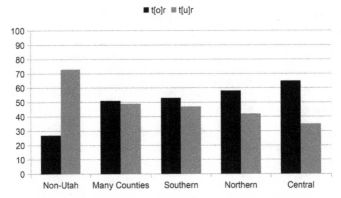

Figure 4.20. Percent of pronunciation responses to *tour* by region raised in.

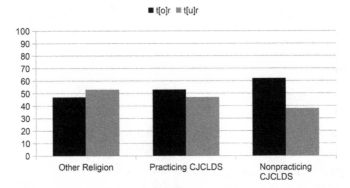

Figure 4.21. Percent of responses to *tour* by religion.

Perhaps the most interesting finding provided by the *tour* question is the influence of religion on the pronunciation, as seen in figure 4.21. There is no statistical difference between the practicing and nonpracticing members of the CJCLDS, while members of other religions differ from both CJCLDS groups. This result indicates that the *t[o]r* pronunciation may be an in-group marker. Although *t[o]r* is far from being isolated to Utah, I feel it is an integral part of Utah English.

ROUTE

Phonetic symbols used in this section

[u] as in sp**oo**k
[aʊ] as in **ou**t

Did the courier take Route 29 while he was routing the documents to their destination, or did the documents go by a different route? While reading the previous sentence, did you pronounce *route* the same way in all three cases? Which ones? Did you say *r[u]t or r[aʊ]t*? About five hundred years ago in what is called the Great Vowel Shift, English words with long [u] vowels shifted to an [aʊ] pronunciation. For example, the earlier pronunciation of *mouse* was *m[u]se*. This variation between *r[u]t* and *r[aʊ]t* shows us that the Great Vowel Shift has never really come to completion.

In the northeastern United States, the *r[u]t* pronunciation is quite common for all the different meanings of *route*.[22] Throughout the entire country, many

Table 4.10. Test Questions and Responses for *Route*

Test Questions	Test Responses
If you are traveling on Route 66, how do you pronounce the high-lighted part of R**out**e?	A t**oo**t B t**ou**t
If you are wondering what the best route to Chicago is, how do you pronounce the highlighted part of r**out**e?	A t**oo**t B t**ou**t
If you work in the post office, you need to route packages to their destination. How do you pronounce the highlighted part of r**out**e?	A t**oo**t B t**ou**t

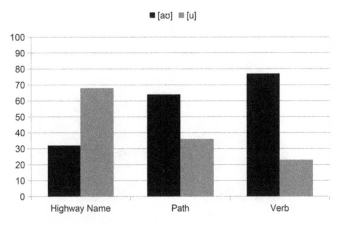

Figure 4.22. Percent of pronunciations matched with the test words according to the meaning of *route*.

people use both pronunciations interchangeably, while others say the word differently depending on the meaning. *Route* is a verb; it is also a noun that means "path" and is a proper noun when used to denote a particular highway. The question we are seeking to answer is how Utahns pronounce *route*. The survey contained three questions designed to elicit pronunciation matches with the three distinct meanings of the word. In general, Utahns prefer r[aʊ]t for the verb and path meanings, but r[u]t in a highway name (figure 4.22).

Route as a Highway Name

Only one variable appears to influence the pronunciation of the highway name to a significant, but not particularly strong degree, and that is education (figure 4.23).[23] Participants with a high school education or less preferred r[aʊ]t slightly more than r[u]t when compared with respondents who had some college experience.

Route Meaning "Path"

The pronunciation of *route* when used to mean "path" is weakly associated with the population of the county the participants resided in.[24] R[aʊ]t was preferred more by participants living in more populated counties (figure 4.24).

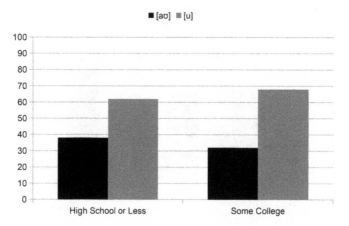

Figure 4.23. Percent of pronunciations matched with the highway name meaning of *route* according to education.

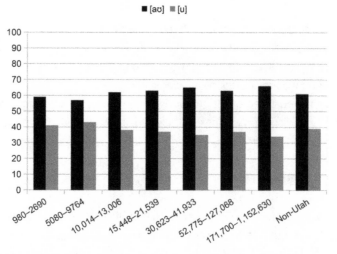

Figure 4.24. Percent of pronunciations matched with *route* meaning "path" according the population of the county of residence.

Route as a Verb

There are a number of interesting, but weak, relationships with the pronunciation of *route* as a verb (table 4.11). In general, younger speakers were more likely to prefer r[u]t for the pronunciation of the verb (figure 4.25), while participants who had lived a greater percent of their life in Utah were less likely to do so

Table 4.11. Statistical Analysis of the Pronunciation Matched with *Route* as a Verb

Predictor	χ^2	df	p	R^2
Age	18.57	1	< .001	.011
Proportion of Life Spent in Utah	4.06	1	0.044	.002
Religion	12.65	2	0.002	.009

McFadden's R^2 = .021

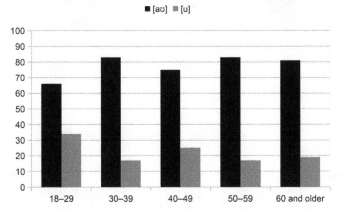

Figure 4.25. Pronunciation matched with *route* as a verb according to age.

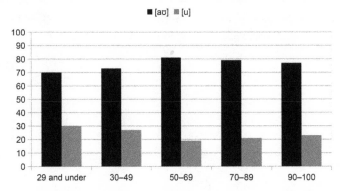

Figure 4.26. Pronunciation matched with *route* as a verb according to percent of the participant's life spent in Utah.

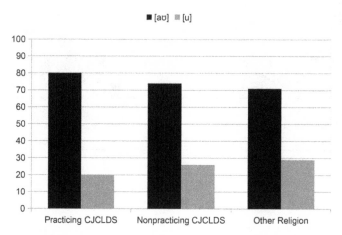

Figure 4.27. Percent of pronunciations matched with *route* as a verb according to religion.

(figure 4.26). The post hoc analysis for religion revealed that the verb *route* was matched with the r[u]t pronunciation less often by practicing members of the CJCLDS when compared with members of other religions (figure 4.27). No other comparisons between religious groups were significant.

As a verb, r[aʊ]t seems to be the older pronunciation for a number of reasons. It is more prevalent among longtime residents, older residents, and the practicing members of the CJCLDS. The youngest Utahns preferred r[u]t more than older groups did, which may signal an apparent-time change in that direction. Future studies will let us know if that has taken place.

Felling Tests in Spanish Fark and Other Shifty Utah Vowels

5

Phonetic symbols used in this section

[l] as in *late*
[eɪ] as in *fake*
[ɛ] as in *bet*
[ʊ] as in *look*
[ʌ] as in *but*

We like to think that language sounds are as solid and unmovable as rock formations on a mountain, when in fact, when viewed over time, the English vowels are more akin to children playing a game of musical chairs. English vowels shift one seat over, push other vowels out of the way, or merge into one in the same chair. About five hundred years ago, the sentence *My mate is going to boot me out of my house* would sound much more like *Me maht is going to boat may oot of me hoose*. Those particular changes are the result of the Great Vowel Shift, which affected most dialects of English to a greater or lesser extent.

It's easy to assume that the game of musical chairs stopped five hundred years ago, while in actuality it is still being played right under our noses. The vowels in the world's many English-speaking regions often don't play the same game their neighbors do. This continuing shift is responsible for much of the regional variation we experience today. Take, for example, the vowels in words such as *love* and *such*. At one point, they had the same vowel as *look* does, [ʊ]. However, in southern England that vowel morphed into [ʌ], and it was that pronunciation that was taken to North America. Northern England and Ireland didn't play this game, which resulted in a dialectal difference: *love* as *l[ʌ]ve* in southern England and *l[ʊ]ve* in Ireland and northern England.

This kind of shifting is still taking place, even in North America. The Northern Cities Shift[1] is what makes people from the Great Lakes region of the

United States say *bag* in a way that sounds more like *beg*. Californians[2] participate in a vowel shift that makes *set* sound more like *sat* and *did* sound more
like *dead*. The vowels in Utah have not escaped these shifts and mergers, as we
shall see.

VOWEL MERGERS BEFORE [l]

The Bible describes a war between the Ephraimites and the Gileadites.[3] At
the time of the war, warring factions didn't wear different uniforms, and the
two nations were not ethnically different, so it wasn't possible to tell the two
groups apart by their appearance. However, the Gileadites knew that Ephraimites couldn't pronounce the *sh* sound, so when they suspected that a person
was an Ephraimite, they would ask the person in question to pronounce the
word *shibboleth*, and if that person said *sibboleth* rather than *shibboleth* they
became proverbial toast.

     This story gave us the term *shibboleth*, which now means a word or pro-
nunciation that marks a person as being from a particular place. Some alleged
shibboleths of Utah English have to do with the merger of different vowels
into a single vowel when that vowel is followed by [l], sounds that linguists call
laterals. In this section I'll discuss the *fill/feel*, *fail/fell*, *pool/pole/pull*, and *hull/
hole/hall* mergers.

     To take one of these as an example, consider the *fail/fell* merger that hap-
pens when the vowel in *fail*, [eɪ], is pronounced as the vowel in *fell*, [ɛ]. This
merger occasionally makes its way into writing, and you may see objects on
the secondhand market listed as *for sell* instead of *for sale*. In the same vein,
one anecdote recalls a conversation with a college student from Utah who
was asked what his career plans were, to which he responded that he was
going into *cells*. The person who inquired assumed that this was an unusual
way for the student to say that he was going to be a biologist, but further
questioning revealed that he intended to be a salesperson; he was going into
sales. It's important to note that this merger mainly happens before laterals because laterals are notorious for modifying the vowels they follow.[4] For
example, a person who says *for sell* would never be heard merging [eɪ] and [ɛ]
before other consonants, that is to say, pronouncing *made* as *med* or *late* as
let. A speaker with the *fail/fell* merger will, however, most likely pronounce all
of the following words with [ɛ] because the vowel in each word is followed by

a lateral: *mail~Mel, whale~well, tail~tell, hail~hell* (the last one making the hymn "We'll Sing All Hail to Jesus' Name" sound sacrilegious to some ears).

Vowel mergers before laterals extend way beyond the borders of Utah. In fact, they are documented across the United States.[5] The idea that the two vowels become identical is probably not technically accurate. These mergers before laterals are more precisely named *near mergers* because, oddly enough, people actually pronounce them in a slightly different manner but can't perceive the distinction in their own speech, nor the speech of others.[6] While I recognize that the mergers I discuss are more precisely *near mergers*, I'll keep it simple and just call them mergers.

I Spelled Melk on My Pellow: **The** *Fill/Fell* **Merger**

Phonetic symbols used in this section

[ɪ] as in p**i**ck
[ɛ] as in p**e**ck

Got melk? Is your pellow too hard? I've often heard these pronunciations pawned off as a sure way to spot a Utahn. People who make this claim have fallen under the spell of the different-means-unique fallacy. Of course, these pronunciations will often fall from the lips of Utahns, but they are far from unique. They actually make up part of the many vowel shifts taking place, such as the Northern Cities Shift,[7] the California Shift,[8] and the Canadian Shift.[9] With all this shifting going on, Utah has not remained untouched. Lillie[10] found that older Utahns pronounce *milk, pillow,* and *hill* with the vowel [ɛ], rather than [ɪ], more than younger Utahns do and that [ɛ] was less common in speakers from northern Utah when compared to speakers from central and southern Utah. Nevertheless, *melk* and *pellow* are poor yardsticks for classifying speakers as hailing from Utah or not.

We Felled the Test: **The** *Fail/Fell* **Merger**

Phonetic symbols used in this section

[ɛ] as in b**e**t
[eɪ] as in b**ai**t

The *Fail/Fell* Merger: Previous Studies

The *fail/fell* merger in Utah has been investigated by quite a few research-ers.[11] There is no question that the merger exists in Utah, but does this mean that when one crosses from Wendover, Nevada, into Wendover, Utah, sud-denly everyone goes to the post office to get their *mel*? No, variation in pro-nunciation just doesn't work that way. When I say that the *fail/fell* merger is a characteristic of Utah English, I mean that you are more likely to hear it in Utah, but that doesn't mean that every Utahn will use it all of the time. It's often the case that usage varies a great deal based on the speaker's gender, age, education, and hometown, as we will see.

What complicates the matter even more is that, as I've already mentioned, the *fail/fell* merger is not uniquely Utahn. For example, I searched for *for sell* in a corpus[12] containing 1.9 billion words from twenty English-speaking countries and found instances of *for sell* in eighteen of the countries. Closer to home, one dialect survey[13] found the *fail/fell* merger sporadically all over the United States. So, if you hear someone say that they *felled* a test, is that a sure *shibboleth* that they are from Utah? No, but it does increase the chances that they may be.

The *Fail/Fell* Merger: Survey Results

In Lillie's study,[14] 42 percent of her participants pronounced the word *sale* as [sɛl]. This pronunciation was more common among younger speakers and those with no college education, as well as among speakers in central Utah. Sarver[15] corroborated these findings but also found more merged vowels

Table 5.1. Test Questions and Responses for the *Fail/Fell* Merger

Test Question	Test Words and Responses

How do you pronounce the highlighted part of the word ___? Like the word ___.	**jai**l
	  A **ja**de
	  B **Je**d
	tail
	  A **te**ch
	  B **ta**ke
	rail
	  A **ra**ke
	  B **wre**ck
	bail
	  A **Be**ck
	  B **ba**ke

among men and rural residents, while Baker and Bowie's study[16] of residents in Utah County reported more mergers among members of the CJCLDS than among those who were not members.

In the present survey, the participants' task was to match their pronunciation of the initial vowel and consonant of the test word with the consonant plus vowel sequence in one of two responses (see table 5.1). Each participant answered only two of the four questions. Only 16 percent matched the test words with the response choice of [ɛ], which is much lower than the 42 percent Lillie observed.

There is a probable explanation for this difference. Lillie's participants merely pronounced the word, while mine had to think about how they said the word and how the responses are pronounced before deciding. This introspection not only requires more effort but also gives more time to participants to reflect on how they may have heard others say the word, or whether they've been told that they say it wrong or that it's a Utah pronunciation, and so on. In other words, the idea that a word has only one proper pronunciation, which is drilled into many students by well-intentioned but linguistically unenlightened English teachers, may have influenced the participants' choice to a much greater extent than merely reading the word out loud would have.

The analysis of the survey data revealed no significant influence of any predictor variable. This finding contrasts with Baker and Bowie,[17] who reported that members of the CJCLDS in Utah County had more *fail/fell* mergers than those of other religions did. I expected to see the same trend, but religion was not a factor here, perhaps because my study included data from all counties in Utah, not just Utah County. Is the *fail/fell* merger a Utahism? Well, in one study,[18] it was one of the pronunciations that people cued in on to distinguish Utahns from other speakers from the western United States. This may indicate that the pronunciation is highly stigmatized, and as a result, the participants may have been reluctant to recognize it in their own speech.

However, there is more to this story than the statistics reveal. In the model, test word and participant were included as random effects. Random effects aren't calculated in the same way as fixed-effect variables like gender, age, and county are. When the random effects of test item and participant are included in a model with no predictor variables, the resulting null model accounts for 95.9 percent of the variance (conditional R^2), which indicates that the differences between test items and individuals is huge. The test items *jail*, *bail*, *rail*, and *tail* were matched with [ɛ] responses in 18 percent, 11 percent, 18 percent, and 17 percent, respectively, of the responses. The small differences between these words makes sense since differences between test items account for only about 1.2 percent of the variance (conditional R^2 = .012), while differences between individual participants account for a whopping 95.3 percent of the variance. The takeaway from all this analysis is that what most affects whether [ɛ] or [eɪ] was chosen is the individual participant. In other words, everyone's got their own way of saying these words, to a certain extent.

How Do You Fill?: The Fill/Feel Merger

Phonetic symbols used in this section

> [i] as in b**ea**t
> [ɪ] as in b**i**t

The Fill/Feel Merger: Previous Studies

A robber walked into a café in Salt Lake City, handed the cashier a bag, and told the cashier to fill it. The cashier complied with his demand by reaching out and feeling the bag. Frustrated, the robber replied, "You've got to be kidding," and left.[19] The would-be holdup was thwarted by what linguists call the *fill/feel* merger.

The two vowels we are talking about are the vowels in *feet* and *fit*. Of course, no one would confuse these words and say something like *"Are your shoes hurting your fit?"* However, I've already mentioned that there is something about laterals that wreak havoc on the vowels that precede them, making the vowels harder to distinguish and often causing them to merge. Such is the case of word pairs like *feel/fill*, *seal/sill*, *steel/still*, and *peel/pill*.

The Fill/Feel Merger: Survey Results

The *fill/feel* merger is certainly something that can be heard in Utah,[20] as the anecdote about the failed robbery attempt illustrates. In one survey, the first vowel in the word *really* was reported to be [ɪ] by 28 percent of the participants.[21] What's more, one study[22] showed that this merger was one of the most salient characteristics of Utah English and that people used it to judge whether or not a speaker was from Utah. Lillie[23] observed the merger more in central Utah followed by southern Utah, followed in turn by northern Utah. While it is true that the *fill/feel* merger can be heard in the state, it is far from unique to the mountains, valleys, and deserts of Utah. One dialect survey shows it to be prevalent in the southern United States and in Texas,[24] but it is in no way limited to the South and is scattered sporadically throughout the rest of the country. In that survey, of the seven respondents in Utah, four merged the vowels to some extent, while three maintained the vowels' distinction.

Instead of counting instances of the *fill/feel* merger in various social groups, Savage[25] set out to get a sense of how this merger is perceived socially. Now, if you just directly ask someone what they think about people who pronounce *heel* as *hill*, a lot of things besides the actual pronunciation are likely to influence their answer, such as, Who is asking? Why? Do they want the "correct" answer? What is their real motive for asking? To avoid this influence, Savage used a match guise task in which listeners heard recordings of speakers and were asked to rate each speaker on how friendly and intelligent they sounded. The trick was that he used recordings that were almost identical except that they varied depending on whether the vowel before the lateral was [i] or [ɪ]. As a result, any differences between the listeners' ratings of the speakers could only be due to the vowel difference. Speakers who used [ɪ] were judged as less friendly and less intelligent than those who pronounced it [i], which speaks to the negative stigma attached to the *fill/feel* merger.

My survey contained four items dealing with the *fill/feel* merger (table 5.2), and each participant responded to only two of them. The only variable that resulted in a significant, but weak, effect was the percent of life the person had spent in the state (figure 5.1).[26] The preference for the vowel [ɪ] increases

Table 5.2. Test Questions and Responses for the *Fill/Feel* Merger

Test Question	Test Words and Responses
How do you pronounce the highlighted part of the word ___? Like the word ___.	**Pee**l
	A **pi**ck
	B **pee**k
	meal
	A **mi**tt
	B **mee**t
	heal
	A **hi**d
	B **hee**d
	deal
	A **di**p
	B **dee**p

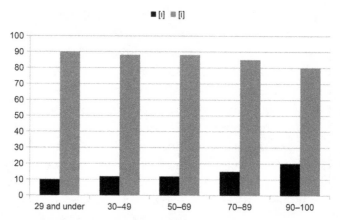

Figure 5.1. Percent of vowels preferred (*y* axis) by the percent of the participant's life that they had spent in Utah (*x* axis).

for those who have spent a larger percentage of their time in the state. Here again 96.3 percent[27] of the variance is due to differences in test items and in the participant's personal speech preferences.

Lillie[28] asked her participants to pronounce the word *heel* and got quite different results. She observed that age and education were related to the pronunciations. The younger speakers produced [ɪ] 34.8 percent of the time, and the older only 18 percent. Those with a college education yielded [ɪ] at a rate of 44 percent, in contrast to those with a high school education at 61.4 percent. These pronunciation rates contrast starkly with the matching task in my study, in which participants matched words to a response—for example, *deal* with the responses ***dee****p* and ***di****p*. Only 17 percent of the responses were matched to words with [ɪ]. Once again, this is probably because Lillie elicited speech, while I asked people to match words with different pronunciations.

The results for the *fill/feel* merger are similar to those of the *fail/fell* merger discussed previously. In both cases, only one variable was significant and it only accounted for a minuscule part of the variance. In the *fill/feel* data, the proportion of life in Utah accounted for only 0.2 percent of the variance.[29] The great majority of the variance was accounted for by the random effects of participant and test item.[30] When the random effect for test item is excluded, the result drops only slightly from .965 to .961. This again strongly points to the major effect that individual participants had above and beyond grouping factors such as where they were born, their gender, their education level, and so on.

The Golf of Mexico

Phonetic symbols used in this section

[ʊ] as in l**oo**k
[u] as in L**u**ke
[ɑ] as in l**o**ck
[ʌ] as in l**u**ck
[o] as in bl**o**ke

The *hall/hull* merger is evident when someone pronounces *golf* and *gulf* with the same vowel or uses that same vowel in both *salt* and *cult*. The *hull/hole* merger makes *cult* and *colt* indistinguishable. The merger involves a shift from [ʌ] to another vowel, so that the word *result* can be heard as *res[ɑ]lt*, *res[o]lt*, or something in between. Likewise, *cult* may be pronounced *c[ɑ]lt, c[o]lt*, or something in between. The movement from [ʌ] to another vowel in both cases is why these two mergers need to be treated together.

With everything that is going on in the United States with vowel shifts and mergers before laterals, you'd think that the *hall/hull* and *hull/hole* mergers would have been investigated more thoroughly. Their existence is only noted in passing in *The Atlas of North American English*,[31] so they merit further study.

In the survey, speakers were asked to match their pronunciation of the test words with the response words (table 5.3). Each participant saw only two of the four questions. Because the vowel in these words can fall somewhere between the vowels in the response words, the participants were told they

Table 5.3. Test Questions and Responses for Words in [ʌl] That Form Part of the *Hull/Hole/Hall* Merger

Test Question	Test Words and Responses
How do you pronounce the highlighted vowel in the word ___? You can choose two words if you feel your pronunciation is close to both words. Like the word ___.	D**u**ll pu**l**se pu**l**p gu**l**f A l**oo**k B L**u**ke C l**o**ck D l**u**ck E bl**o**ke

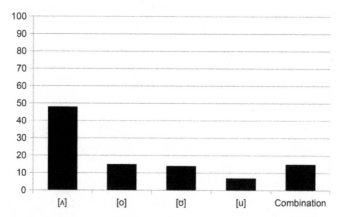

Figure 5.2. Percent of pronunciations matched to the test words with the *hull/hole/hall* merger.

could choose more than one response. These responses are marked as *combination* in figure 5.2. Note that no one chose [ɑ] (*lock*) as their only response. This vowel was always chosen along with another vowel, which indicates some intermediate pronunciation that falls between [ɑ] and another vowel. As you can see, there is a great deal of variation, and the results of the statistical analysis help sort out what caused that variation (table 5.4).

For this analysis I reduced the five responses in figure 5.2 to only two: [ʌ] versus all others. This was justified for a number of reasons. First, including so many values tended to make the statistical software choke. Second, the interpretation of such a model would be extremely complex. Third, the real question I was interested in is what variables are related to conservation of [ʌ] versus the use of some other vowel in its place.

Table 5.4. Statistical Results of the *Hull/Hole/Hall* Merger

Predictor	χ^2	df	p	R^2
Age	51.96	1	< .001	.030
Gender	6.64	1	0.010	.003
Born and Raised in Utah	5.77	1	0.016	.006
Religion	13.52	3	0.004	.017

Marginal R^2 = .056
Conditional R^2 = .427

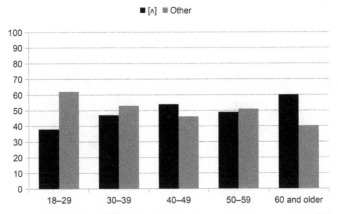

Figure 5.3. Percent of pronunciations matched to words with [ʌ] in the *hull/hole/hall* merger by age.

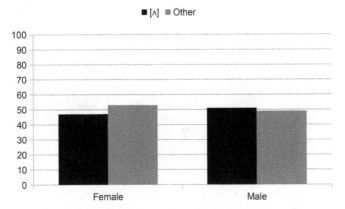

Figure 5.4. Percent of pronunciations matched to words with [ʌ] in the *hull/hole/hall* merger by gender.

The analysis revealed that younger people were more likely to match pronunciations other than [ʌ] to the test words (figure 5.3). This apparent time trend suggests that [ʌ] may become a less common pronunciation for these words in the future. The fact that women tend to be on the forefront of linguistic changes could be taken as support for the idea that the trend away from [ʌ] may happen in the future (figure 5.4).

Dividing the state into regions didn't fit the model as well as simply separating the participants who were born and raised in Utah from those who weren't

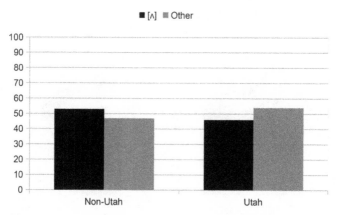

Figure 5.5. Percent of pronunciations matched to words with [ʌ] in the *hull/hole/hall* merger by being born and raised in Utah.

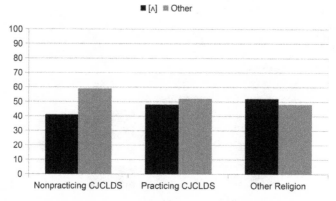

Figure 5.6. Percent of pronunciations matched to words with [ʌ] in the *hull/hole/hall* merger by religion.

(figure 5.5). It appears that the shift away from [ʌ] may be more advanced in born-and-bred Utahns.

Religious groups also exhibit differences in their preferences for [ʌ] and other pronunciations (figure 5.6). When the three groups are compared, the only significant difference between them is that members of other faith preferred [ʌ] more than nonpracticing CJCLDS members. In their study of speakers in Utah County, Baker and Bowie (2010) found no evidence for merger of [o] with [ʌ] in either members of the CJCLDS or those who were not. They did not, however, compare practicing and nonpracticing members of the CJCLDS, as I have.

The first conclusion we can make about the *hull/hole/hall* merger is that [ʌ] doesn't move to [ɑ], which means that the merger is really a merger between *hull* and *hole*, or between *hull* and *who'll*, or between [ʌ] and [ʊ], but that *hall* is not involved. Many speakers matched [ʌ] words with [ʊ], [u], and [o] words (and combinations of the vowels in those words), so the resulting vowel must fall in the neighborhood of [ʊ], [u], and [o]. Exactly what that vowel is needs to be determined by examining acoustic data. The second conclusion is that movement away from [ʌ] is a characteristic of Utah English. Whether it is also a characteristic of English in other states needs to be investigated as well.

The Swimming Pull: Pool/Pole/Pull **Merger**

Phonetic symbols used in this section

[o] as in n**o**te
[u] as in l**oo**p
[ʊ] as in l**oo**k
[ʌ] as in l**u**ck

A few years ago, I attended a city council meeting in my small town in Utah County. Among other items on the agenda, the council discussed a competition in the upcoming county fair in which each town would decorate a b[ʌ]l. The b[ʌ]l from each city would be judged and the best one awarded a prize. I imagined a table covered with bowls from each city, until, later on in the discussion, a council member mentioned that the objects to be judged would be made of two-by-four planks of wood. How do you make a round bowl out of two-by-fours? I must have misunderstood, so I focused more intently on the word in question and at times heard something like b[o]l. Finally, the context of one sentence made me realize that the competition was between *bulls* made of planks, not *bowls*. In that moment I realized that I was not the only one confused by the discussion because many members of the audience let out a collective *oh* with an accompanying shake of the head when they too finally caught on.

The *Pool/Pole/Pull* Merger: **Previous Research**

This tripartite merger involves the merger or near merger of the vowels [ʊ, o, u] before laterals. Not everyone merges all three, which is why they are often talked about as mergers between only two vowels: *pull/pool*, *pool/pole*, and *pull/pole*. The *pool/pull* merger, while found sporadically around the United States, has a large concentration in Pennsylvania and Indiana.[32] However, none of the seven Utahns in the *Atlas of North American English* survey merged these vowels; instead, they maintained the distinction. However, earlier work on Utah English did find a merger in progress in the state.[33]

In a survey conducted in 1997,[34] 21.5 percent of the participants pronounced *pool* as p[ʊ]l, and it was the older group that demonstrated more merger. This contrasts with Sarver's study[35] in which people aged twenty-five or older did not merge *pull* and *pool*, while those under twenty-five did. In contrast to the *pull* and *pool* merger, Sarver reported that *pull* and *pole* were merged regardless of age or the size of the city the respondents lived in. The merger between all three words—*pull*, *pool*, and *pole*—occurred only in the group of respondents who were eighteen to twenty-five years old. These vowels differ on a number of features, and Sarver found more merging based on the frontness of the vowel, that is, how far forward the tongue is during the articulation of the vowel. When only the frontness of the vowels was considered, men, people with college degrees, and city dwellers merged all three to a greater extent.

The *Pool/Pole/Pull* Merger: Survey Results for [ul]

In this part of the survey the participants matched the vowels in test words with the vowels in the response choices. Each participant saw only two of the four test words, and they were allowed to choose more than one response if they felt their pronunciation was close to the vowel in more than one of the response choices. The three most common responses were [u] 62 percent, [ʊ] 23 percent, and a combination of [ʊ] and [u] 10 percent. The remaining 5 percent of responses consisted of other vowels and combinations of vowels.[36] In the statistical analysis, this was simplified to [u], [ʊ], and other.

Survey Results for [ul]: [u] Responses versus All Others

The question asked in this analysis was what variables are related to test words with [u] being matched to responses with [u] versus test words being matched to any other response. Matching with [u] indicates no vowel merger. This is contrasted with [u] matched to responses with other vowels that are indicative of a merger (table 5.6). The influence of age is apparent in figure 5.7, where older speakers retain [u] more than younger speakers, who merge [u] with another vowel to a greater extent.[37] One factor that negatively affects merging

Table 5.5. Test Questions and Responses for Words in [ul] That Form Part of the *Pool/Pole/Pull* Merger

Test Question	Test Words and Responses
How do you pronounce the highlighted vowel in the word ___? You can choose two words if you feel your pronunciation is close to both words. Like the word ___.	sch**oo**l c**oo**l r**u**le p**oo**l A l**oo**k B L**u**ke C l**o**ck D l**u**ck E bl**o**ke

[u] with another vowel is the participants' degree of education (figure 5.8). Fewer mergers were chosen by the more educated participants. If merging is socially stigmatized, perhaps it is eschewed by those with a postsecondary education. Although older speakers were more likely to have achieved a higher degree of education, there was no significant interaction of age and education, so the influence of age and education on merging are independent of each other.

The region the participants were raised in is also significant (figure 5.9). When the groups are compared to each other statistically, the data show that the non-Utah group chose [u] significantly more than those raised in many different counties or outside of the limited Wasatch Front did. (You may want to go back to figure 1.2 in chapter 1 to see what counties are included in the limited and extended Wasatch Front.) Similarly, people who were raised in the limited Wasatch Front preferred [u] more than the participants who were

Table 5.6. Statistical Results of the *Pool/Pole/Pull* Merger: [u] Responses versus All Others

Predictor	χ^2	df	p	R^2
Age	4.72	1	0.030	.002
Education	18.53	1	<.001	.023
Region Raised in—Limited Wasatch Front	21.74	3	<.001	.025
Region of Residence—Extended Wasatch Front	11.16	1	<.001	.019
Religion	12.70	2	0.002	.014

Marginal R^2 = .062
Conditional R^2 = .386

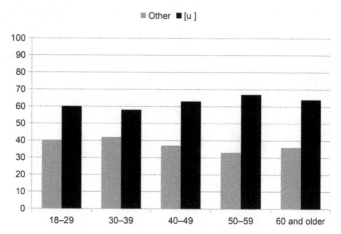

Figure 5.7. The merger of [u] in the *pool/pole/pull* merger: Percent of test items matched to [u] or another vowel by age.

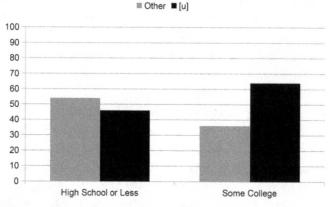

Figure 5.8. The merger of [u] in the *pool/pole/pull* merger: Percent of test items matched to [u] or another vowel by education.

raised either outside of the limited Wasatch Front or in many different counties did. The data on where the participants currently live (figure 5.10) reveal that residents outside of the extended Wasatch Front preferred [u] less than members of the other two groups did.[38]

How does religion play into this? Membership in a tightly knit community such as the CJCLDS can provide an environment in which changes can be quickly adopted and transmitted. However, that same sense of community

Other ■ [u]

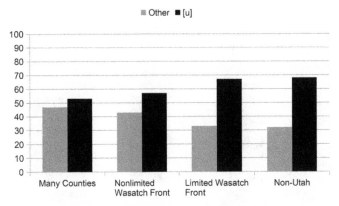

Figure 5.9. The merger of [u] in the *pool/pole/pull* merger: Percent of test items matched to [u] or another vowel by region raised in.

■ [u] Other

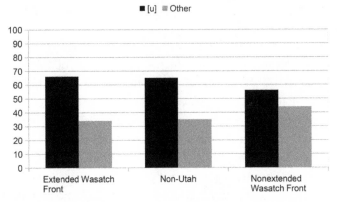

Figure 5.10. The merger of [u] in the *pool/pole/pull* merger: Percent of test items matched to [u] or another vowel by region of residence.

may resist change if it is viewed as an out-group characteristic. The post hoc analysis shows practicing members of the CJCLDS merging much less than members of other religions did, while there are no differences between the other and nonpracticing groups (figure 5.11), meaning that the merger or lack thereof is a group marker.

On one hand, merging [u] into another vowel may be considered a more recent change because it is more common among younger speakers. On the other hand, you'd expect newer changes to be more advanced in more urban areas, which is not the case.

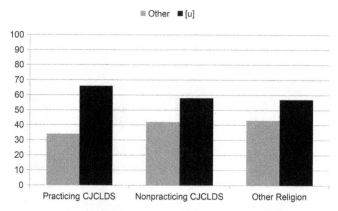

Figure 5.11. The merger of [u] in the *pool/pole/pull* merger: Percent of test items matched to [u] or another vowel by religion.

Survey Results for [ul]: [ʊ] Responses versus All Others

Since the most common vowel that [u] merged into was [ʊ], I wanted to see what variables are related to the choice of this vowel versus all others. The region of the state that the participants were raised in or presently reside in were both significant, although the best-fitting grouping of counties was not into north, central, and south but into limited Wasatch Front and nonlimited Wasatch Front (table 5.7).

The effect of either residing in or having grown up in a region is very similar. Statistically speaking, participants who either grew up in the limited Wasatch Front or presently reside there are less likely to have matched test words with [u] to response words with [ʊ], when compared with those who were raised or reside outside of the limited Wasatch Front. Additionally, the participants raised

Table 5.7. Statistical Results of the *Pool/Pole/Pull* Merger: Matching Test Items with [u] to Responses with [ʊ] versus All Others

Predictor	χ^2	df	p	R^2
County Raised in—Limited Wasatch Front	20.8	3	< .001	.027
County of Residence—Limited Wasatch Front	12.2	1	< .001	.024
Religion	30.2	2	< .001	.019

Marginal R^2 = .058
Conditional R^2 = .341

outside of the state also preferred a response other than [ʊ], when compared with those raised outside of the limited Wasatch Front (figures 5.12 and 5.13).

Participants who were raised in the limited Wasatch Front don't differ from those who were raised outside of Utah or who were raised in many counties. Similarly, participants residing in the limited Wasatch Front chose responses with [ʊ] to the same degree as those who presently live outside of Utah. Once again, this information leads me to believe that any future study that

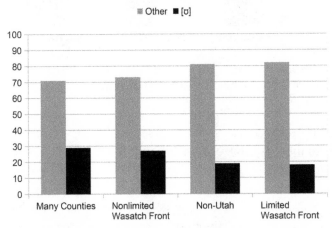

Figure 5.12. The merger of [u] in the *pool/pole/pull* merger: Percent of test items matched to [ʊ] or another vowel by region raised in.

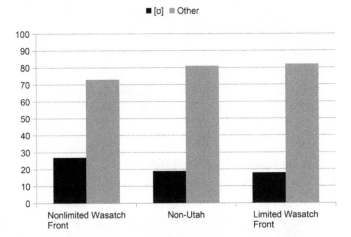

Figure 5.13. The merger of [u] in the *pool/pole/pull* merger: Percent of test items matched to [ʊ] or another vowel by region of residence.

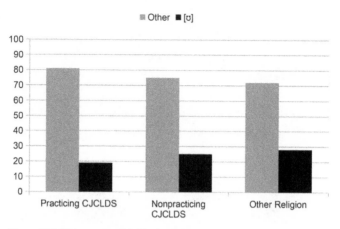

Figure 5.14. The merger of [u] in the *pool/pole/pull* merger: Percent of test items matched to [ʊ] or another vowel by religion.

compares non-Utah speakers with Utah speakers will find that Utahns who have ties to the Wasatch Front will probably be more similar to non-Utahns than will the Utahns from outside of the Wasatch Front. This is a dissertation waiting to happen.

Religion also plays a part here, as is seen in figure 5.14. The only groups that differ significantly in their use of [ʊ] are the practicing members of the CJCLDS and the members of other religions. Again, if we consider the *pool/ pole/pool* merger to be a change in progress, fewer practicing members of the CJCLDS have jumped on that merger's bandwagon. Nonpracticing members, in contrast, pattern with members of other faiths.

While in previous surveys age has generally been a significant predictor of merging, it is conspicuously absent here. In contrast, Sarver[39] observed *pool* merging with *pull* among the younger residents of Utah County. However, in Lillie's statewide study,[40] merging was more common in the older participants.

The *Pool/Pole/Pull* Merger: Survey Results for [ol]

The topic of this section is the extent to which *pole* words have merged with *pool* and *pull* words. The survey participants were given two of the four test words and asked to match the vowel in the test words containing [o] to the vowels in the response words (table 5.8). They could choose more than one response if they felt their pronunciation was close to several vowels.[41]

Table 5.8. Test Questions and Responses for Words in [ol] That Form Part of the *Pool/Pole/Pull* Merger

Test Question	Test Words and Responses
How do you pronounce the highlighted vowel in the word ___? You can choose two words if you feel your pronunciation is close to both words. Like the word ___.	p<u>o</u>le g<u>oa</u>l m<u>o</u>le c<u>oa</u>l A l<u>oo</u>k B L<u>u</u>ke C l<u>o</u>ck D l<u>u</u>ck E bl<u>o</u>ke

The great majority of the participants chose response words with [o] 86 percent, while 4 percent chose [ʊ] and 3 percent [ɑ]; the remaining 7 percent were spread across eighteen other vowels and vowel combinations. When cases of [o] were contrasted with all others combined, the only significant variable was age[42] (figure 5.15). Sarver also noted the influence of age.[43] In his survey of Utah County, the participants between eighteen and twenty-four years of age merged all three vowels: *pool/pull/pole.* Yet, sixteen years after Sarver's study it is still the younger demographic that gives the *pole* category

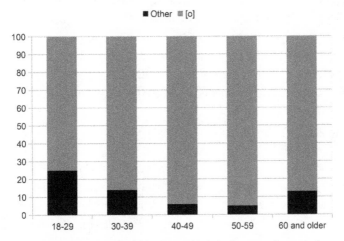

Figure 5.15. The merger of [o] in the *pool/pole/pull* merger: Percent of test items matched to [o] or another vowel by age.

Table 5.9. Test Questions and Responses for Words in [ʊl] That Form Part of the *Pool/Pole/Pull* Merger

Test Question	Test Words and Responses
How do you pronounce the highlighted vowel in the word ___?	P**u**ll
	f**u**ll
You can choose two words if you feel your pronunciation is close to both words.	w**oo**l
	b**u**ll
Like the word ___.	A l**oo**k
	B L**u**ke
	C l**o**ck
	D l**u**ck
	E bl**o**ke

of words a pronunciation other than [o], not the group of participants age thirty to thirty-nine, as an age-apparent time change would have predicted.

While age is significant, it accounts for only 0.2 percent of the variance; the bulk is due to the test items and individual participants. These results make me conclude that the *pole/pull* merger, while it is catching on among the youngest demographic, is not an important characteristic of the English spoken in Utah, although it may be moving in that direction.

The *Pool/Pole/Pull* Merger: Survey Results for [ʊl]

In this part of the survey, each participant matched the vowel [ʊ] in two test words to the vowels in the response words. Once again, participants could choose more than one response when they perceived that their own pronunciation fell between the vowels in one or more of the response choices. The most common choices were [ʊ] 31 percent, [ʌ] 24 percent, [o] 14 percent, and [u] 14 percent. The remaining 17 percent consisted of seventeen different vowels and vowel combinations. The fact that 69 percent of the matches were not with [ʊ] is clear evidence that this vowel has been merged on a wide-scale level in Utah English.

The vowels [ʊ], [o], and [u] are expected outcomes in a merger between the *pool/pole/pull* vowels, but here [ʌ] was a common choice, so maybe we need to extend the *pool/pole/pull* merger to include *dull*. (Unfortunately, we can't give it a nice symmetrical name such as the *pool/pole/pull/p[ʌ]ll* merger because there is no *p[ʌ]ll* in English.)

Table 5.10. Statistical Results of the *Pool/Pole/Pull* Merger: Matching Test Items with [ʊ] to Responses with [ʊ] versus All Others

Predictor	χ^2	df	p	R^2
Age	14.15	1	< .001	.006
Region Raised in—3 Regions	22.94	4	< .001	.013
Region of Residence—Extended Wasatch Front	7.21	2	.027	.004

Marginal R^2 = .023
Conditional R^2 = .247

Survey Results for [ʊl]: [ʊ] Responses versus All Others

The statistical analysis points to three associated variables that are important here: age, the region the participants were raised in, and the population of the county they reside in (table 5.10). The effect of age, as you can see in figure 5.16, is quite clear; merging [ʊ] with another vowel is much more common than not merging. It is the older participants who demonstrate less merging and the younger speakers who have taken the merger further along.

The region of the state the participants were raised in was important as well (figure 5.17). The post hoc analysis indicates that those raised outside of the state preferred [ʊ] more than those raised in northern and central Utah did. There was also a trend[44] for central Utahns to prefer [ʊ] less often than

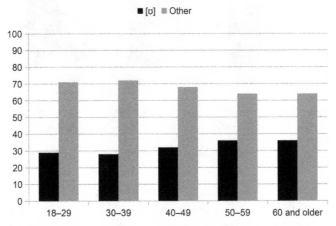

Figure 5.16. The merger of [ʊ] in the *pool/pole/pull* merger: Percent of test items matched to [ʊ] or another vowel by age.

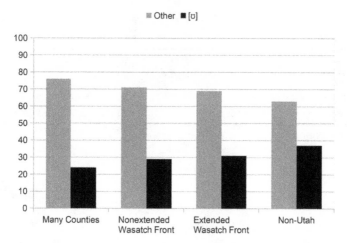

Figure 5.17. The merger of [ʊ] in the *pool/pole/pull* merger: Percent of test items matched to [ʊ] or another vowel by region raised in.

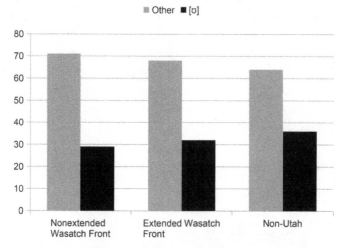

Figure 5.18. The merger of [ʊ] in the *pool/pole/pull* merger: Percent of test items matched to [ʊ] or another vowel by region of residence—extended Wasatch Front.

northern Utahns. This points to central Utah as the focal point for the merger of [ʊ] with another vowel. The influence of the region the participants reside in appears in figure 5.18. Although this predictor was significant, the post hoc indicates no difference between the three regions.

Table 5.11. Statistical Results of the *Pool/Pole/Pull* Merger: Matching Test Items with [ʊ] to Responses with [u] versus All Others

Predictor	χ^2	df	p	R^2
Age	13.98	1	< .001	.011
Education	9.53	1	0.002	.006

Marginal R^2 = .018
Conditional R^2 = .371

Survey Results for [ʊl]: [u] Responses versus All Others

Ten percent of the responses demonstrated a merger between [ʊ] and [u], such as pronouncing *pull* as *pool* with the vowel [u]. The responses were influenced by participants' age and educational level (table 5.11). The [u] response was favored by older speakers and those with a high school education or less (figures 5.19 and 5.20). Although the influence of religion wasn't significant in my data, Baker and Bowie[45] observed that more respondents who were not members of the CJCLDS perceived the [ʊ] in words such as *pull* to be closer to [u] than did members of the CJCLDS.

Survey Results for [ʊl]: [o] Responses versus All Others

Although merging [ʊ] with [o] occurred in 14 percent of the responses, no variables were found to be associated with this merger.

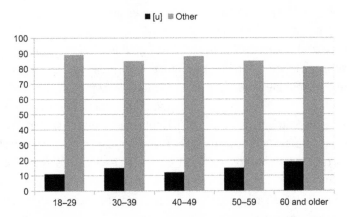

Figure 5.19. The merger of [ʊ] in the *pool/pole/pull* merger: Percent of test items matched to [u] or another vowel by age.

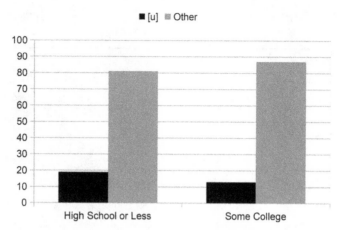

Figure 5.20. The merger of [ʊ] in the *pool/pole/pull* merger: Percent of test items matched to [u] or another vowel by education.

Survey Results for [ʊl]: [ʌ] Responses versus All Others

Nearly a fourth of the responses involved a merger between [ʊ] and [ʌ]. Two predictors influenced matching the test words to [ʌ]. The first is gender (table 5.12), although the effect size is extremely small. Women preferred the vowel [ʌ] more than men did (figure 5.21). The second is the region of residence (figure 5.22). Those residing outside the state chose [ʌ] less often than Utahns residing in all three regions, and there is no difference between the choices of the participants residing in any of the three regions.

Summary of the Survey Results of the *Pool/Pole/Pull* Merger

Perhaps all the charts and tables and statistics I've presented on the *pool/pole/ pull* merger seem piecemeal, so let me tie them together. *Pole* is the easiest to summarize. Only 14 percent of the time did the participants match the [o] in a test word with any other vowel except [o] in a response item. Younger participants preferred responses other than [o] more than older participants did. This result leads me to conclude that we can exclude *pole* from the *pool/ pole/pull* merger, even while recognizing that the age data suggest it may gain steam in the future. It is more precise to consider Utah a place where *pool* and *pull* merge, but not *pole*.

The [u] vowel in *pool*, on the other hand, was more often merged with another vowel by younger speakers, the less educated, and people who were

Table 5.12. Statistical Results of the *Pool/Pole/Pull* Merger: Matching Test Items with [ʊ] to Responses with [ʌ] versus All Others

Predictor	χ^2	df	p	R^2
Gender	6.74	1	.009	.004
Region of Residence—3 Regions	12.28	4	.006	.008

Marginal R^2 = .011
Conditional R^2 = .472

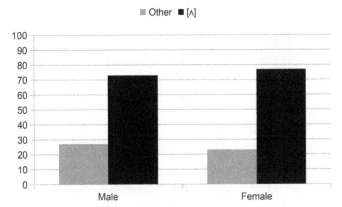

Figure 5.21. The merger of [ʊ] in the *pool/pole/pull* merger: Percent of test items matched to [ʌ] or another vowel by gender.

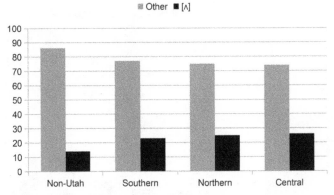

Figure 5.22. The merger of [ʊ] in the *pool/pole/pull* merger: Percent of test items matched to [ʌ] or another vowel by region of residence.

raised or reside outside of the limited Wasatch Front. The merger is also more prominent in participants who were nonpracticing members of the CJCLDS and members of other religious groups.

While [u] remained unmerged in 62 percent of the responses, when it did merge it was merged principally with [ʊ] at a rate of 23 percent. More specifically, the merger of [u] into the [ʊ] of *pull* was done more by those participants who were raised or were residing outside of the limited Wasatch Front, and by members of other religions compared to practicing members of the CJCLDS.

As far as the *pull* part of the equation is concerned, the [ʊ] vowel stayed unmerged in only 31 percent of the response choices, while the most common merger was with [ʌ] (24 percent), followed by [o] (14 percent) and [u] (14 percent). Participants who merged [ʊ] with another vowel were younger speakers, those from the central part of the state, and people residing in less populated counties. No significant predictor variables arose from the statistical analysis of what influenced the merger of [ʊ] into [o]. However, women merged [ʊ] into [ʌ] more often than men did. Those who merged [ʊ] more often with [u] were the less educated and the older participants.

Another way to summarize these data is to consider how many individual participants produced mergers. To calculate this, I first removed the 139 participants who did not respond to at least one of three *pool/pole/pull* questions. Figure 5.23 gives the percentage of participants who showed mergers for each vowel. For example, 31 percent of the participants showed signs of two mergers: [ʊ] into another vowel and [u] into another vowel. The most telling number is that only about 7 percent of participants merged no vowel with any

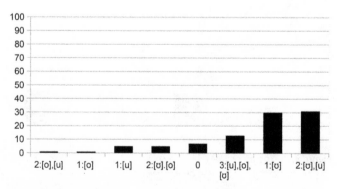

Figure 5.23. Percent of participants who merged the indicated vowels with some other vowel in at least one test item.

other. The fact that 93 percent did merge to some extent is a clear indication that the *pool/pole/pull* merger is well underway in Utah, and that it is a defining characteristic of Utah English.

On the other extreme, only 13 percent of participants merged all three of the pre-lateral vowels with some other vowel at least once, which tells us that a three-way merger is unusual in the state. As I discussed previously, only 14 percent of the participants merged test items with *pool*-type vowels at least once. When this information is taken together with the fact that [o] is merged with another vowel much less than [u] and [ʊ] are, we can conclude that *pole* mergers are not particularly prevalent in Utah. In contrast, [u] and [ʊ] were merged with each other or with other vowels by 61 percent of the participants, meaning that the *pull* and *pool* parts of the *pool/pole/pull* merger are most definitely a characteristic of Utah speech.

OTHER VOWEL MERGERS

Sticking Pen or Writing Pin?: The *Pin/Pen* Merger

Phonetic symbols used in this section

[ɛ] as in b**e**t
[ɪ] as in b**i**t

The *pin/pen* merger is responsible for making these word pairs, among others, identical: *him/hem, kin/Ken, windy/Wendy*. This merger is widespread in the southern United States, and if you ask someone there for a *pen* or *pin* they may ask for clarification: "Do you want a writing p[ɪ]n or a sticking p[ɪ]n?" Now, Utah is far from the South, but this merger is often brought up in discussions of Utah English. Of the seven Utah respondents in one survey,[46] six kept the two words distinct. Only 13 percent of Lillie's participants pronounced *pen* with an [ɪ],[47] and this pronunciation was more frequent among her older cohort. Baker and Bowie[48] carried out a perception study with people from Utah County. The participants who were not members of the CJCLDS did not distinguish the [ɛ] and [ɪ] vowels before *n* as much as members of the CJCLDS did.

In my survey, the participants responded to two of the questions in table 5.13, and 87 percent of the matched responses were with unmerged

Table 5.13. Test Questions and Responses for Questions Involving the *Pin/Pen* Merger

Test Question	Test Words and Responses

How do you pronounce the highlighted part of the word ___? Like the word ___.	**Pe**n
	  A **pe**ck
	  B **pi**ck
	hem
	  A **he**ck
	  B **hi**ck
	empty
	  A **F** (The letter "F")
	  B **if**
	many
	  A **mi**tt
	  B **me**t

[ɛ], while only 13 percent were with [ɪ], which is indicative of a merger. Three variables influenced the merger or lack of merger (table 5.14). Participants with high school studies or less merged more than those with some college education (figure 5.24).

The region that participants were raised in or reside in was also a significant predictor (figures 5.25 and 5.26), and the post hoc test shows significantly less merging taking place among those raised or residing in the extended Wasatch Front[49] when compared with those raised outside of it. Consistent with Baker and Bowie,[50] non-CJCLDS members merged more [ɛ] vowels into [ɪ] than did practicing members (figure 5.27). In sum, this merger is not terribly frequent in the Beehive State, which is why I am reluctant to include it as a prominent feature of Utah English.

Table 5.14. Statistical Results for the *Pin/Pen* Merger

Predictor	χ^2	df	p	R^2
Education	7.09	1	0.008	.017
Region Raised in—Extended Wasatch Front	23.80	3	<.001	.055
Region of Residence—Extended Wasatch Front	15.26	2	<.001	.048
Religion	15.19	3	0.002	.029

Marginal R^2 = .099
Conditional R^2 = .551

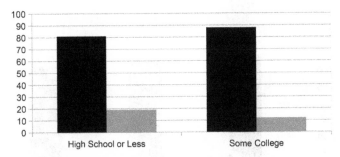

Figure 5.24. Percent of responses matched to vowels in the *pin/pen* merger by education.

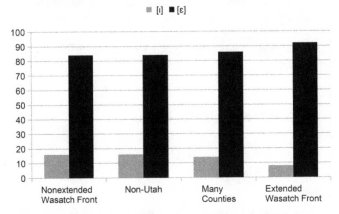

Figure 5.25. Percent of responses matched to vowels in the *pin/pen* merger by region raised in.

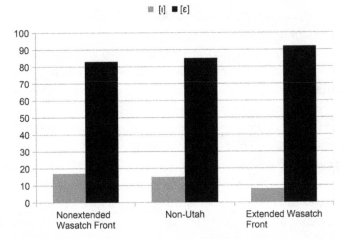

Figure 5.26. Percent of responses matched to vowels in the *pin/pen* merger by region of residence.

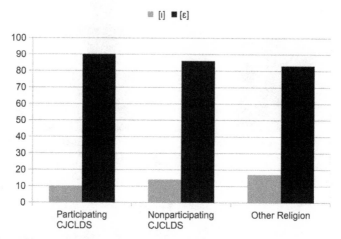

Figure 5.27. Percent of responses matched to vowels in the *pin/pen* merger by religion.

I'm Dawn Not Don: The *Caught/Cot* Merger

Phonetic symbols used in this section

[ɑ] as in *f**a**ther*
[ɔ] as in *s**aw*** (eastern U.S. and British pronunciation)

Imagine the linguistic situation in the western United States during the nine-teenth century. In search of land, freedom, and gold, people flocked to the West from many different regions of the East, as well as from several English-speaking countries. The various dialects of the native-English immigrants were mixed in with the nonnative accents spoken by the Greeks, Italians, and Scandi-navians. Yet, in the course of just a few generations, those varieties of English coalesced into the western dialects as we now know them.

In communities that were originally comprised of many different dialects, we have observed the formation of a leveled dialect.[51] In general, this involves a dialect simplified to the lowest common denominator. As an example, consider the words *Mary, merry,* and *marry*. In some dialects these words have three distinct vowels. In others, two of the words are pronounced identically. In yet other dialects, all three words use the same vowel sound. Dialect leveling pre-dicts that in places where people with many dialects form a new dialect, the newly formed variety will simplify the distinction so that a single pronunciation for *Mary, merry,* and *marry,* for example, will be homophones. This was one result of dialect leveling in the western United States.

Many English dialects make a distinction between the vowels [ɑ] and [ɔ]. In those dialects *dawn, caught, bought, walk,* and *stalk,* contain [ɔ], while *Don, cot, bot, wok,* and *stock* have [ɑ]. In the western United States, this distinction has been leveled so that for most westerners [ɔ] never contrasts with [ɑ].[52] This is known as the *caught/cot* merger. Bowie[53] listened for the merger in the recorded speech of Utahns born between 1847 and 1896. Overall, the merger was evident in 60 percent of the cases, but speakers born later merged more, and the merger has continued to dominate until the present day. Along with other westerners, most Utahns don't distinguish between [ɑ] and [ɔ].

However, the situation is a bit more complex because the *caught/cot* merger is, in actuality, a near merger. This means that although speakers claim to say *caught* and *cot* the same way, when you examine their pronunciations acoustically, there are subtle differences. For example, Sarver's acoustic study,[54] which was done in Utah County, found more mergers among older speakers. In an earlier study of the *caught/cot* merger,[55] six speakers were recorded pronouncing words involved in the merger, and they all produced acoustically distinct vowels for pairs such as *walk/wok* and *caught/cot.*

Researchers have tested the effect of religion on pronunciation in Utah County. Although merging was the norm there,[56] practicing and nonpracticing members of the CJCLDS merged to the same degree, but there was a difference—not in the degree of merger but in the vowel that resulted from the merger. Nonpracticing CJCLDS members had vowels pronounced with a lower tongue position than practicing members did. A difference was also observed in the merged vowel when members and nonmembers of the CJCLDS were contrasted.[57]

How Utahns perceive the merger or lack thereof was measured in a matched guise experiment.[58] The participants heard recordings of a number of speakers and judged each speaker on several positive personality characteristics such as honest, friendly, educated, and dependable. The same speakers were recorded using both [ɑ] and [ɔ] in one recording, and only [ɑ] in another. The participants were told that each recording was of a different speaker, so any differences in the listeners' ratings must be due, not to individual vocal characteristics, but to the merger or lack of merger in the recording. The recordings in which the speakers maintained the [ɑ] and [ɔ] distinction received less favorable ratings. This is evidence that merging the vowels was considered the more prestigious form of speech. In sum, Utahns pronounce [ɑ] and [ɔ] somewhat differently although they don't perceive the distinction. They also feel that merging is the more prestigious form of speech.

Grocery Begs: *Bag* Raising and the *Beck/Bake* Merger

Phonetic symbols used in the section

> [æ] as in b*a*t
> [ɛ] as in b*e*t
> [eɪ] as in b*ai*t

Years ago, when I was a college student, I spent the summer working in a KFC in rural Colorado. One day, a coworker of mine from Detroit asked me to give her the r*[eɪ]g*. I stood there staring at her with a blank face trying to understand what *rake* she could possibly be referring to. I asked her to repeat her question twice more. On the second try I heard r*[ɛ]g*, which didn't match anything in my mental dictionary either. Finally, with obvious frustration painted on her face, she shifted her pronunciation into something I could grasp: r*[æ]g*. I gave her the rag I was using to clean the countertop, and she stormed off while I was left to ponder what I would later learn was referred to as [æ] raising, or *bag* raising, in American English.

In one large-scale study,[59] words such as *maggot*, *drag*, and *wagon* were often judged as having raised vowels, such as [ɛ], by speakers in the northernmost part of the United States and extending into Canada. In Utah, raised vowels were not very prevalent. Nevertheless, in another study, members of the CJCLDS shifted [æ] to [ɛ] more than nonmembers did.[60] In southern Alberta, the opposite was observed: CJCLDS members shifted less than non-members did.[61] As far as the raising of [ɛ] to [eɪ] is concerned, 35 percent of Utahns pronounced *Craig* with [eɪ] in an earlier study.[62]

A number of items in my survey were included to test these mergers (table 5.15). Participants saw two *Beck/bake* merger questions and two *bag* raising questions. As far as *bag* raising is concerned, 97 percent of the matches were to words with [æ], indicating an almost complete lack of merger. The remainder contained the raised vowels [ɛ] (1 percent) and [eɪ] (2 percent).

Table 5.15. Test Questions and Responses for the *Bag* Raising and *Beck/Bake* Merger

Test Question for the Beck/Bake Merger	Test Words and Responses
How do you pronounce the highlighted part of the word ___? Like the word ___.	**Be**g A **Be**ck B **ba**ke **le**g A **le**t B **la**te **pe**gboard A **Pe**z B **pay**s **pre**gnant A **pre**s. (president) B **pray**s

Test Question for *Bag* Raising	Test Words and Responses
How do you pronounce the highlighted part of the word ___? Like the word ___.	**Ba**g A **be**t B **ba**t C **bai**t **la**g A **lai**d B **la**d C **le**d **fla**g A **fla**sh B **fle**sh C **fla**ys **ga**g A **gue**ss B **ga**s C **ga**ys

The statistical analysis identified no predictors as significantly related to the variation. *Bag* raising is just not part of Utah English.

In a similar way, 85 percent of the responses to the questions designed to test the *Beck/bake* merger were [ɛ], which indicates a general lack of merger. The remaining 15 percent of matches were to raised [eɪ]. Age was the only significant predictor.[63] As you can see in figure 5.28, raising into [eɪ] was done more by the older participants and was almost unknown among the youngest which suggests an uncommon merger that is dying in the state.

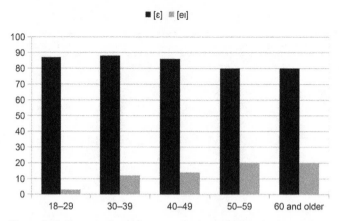

Figure 5.28. Percent of responses matched to vowels in the *beck/bake* merger by age.

As far as *bag* raising is concerned, only 3 percent of the participants chose something other than the unmerged [æ], and no predictor was flagged as significant in the statistical analysis.

These findings corroborate Stanley's,[64] in that *Beck/bake* mergers are more frequent than *bag* raising. While others[65] reported an influence of religion on these mergers, the data from this survey are contradictory because religion was not a significant factor. These mergers don't appear to play a significant role in Utah English, in my completely objective and totally unbiased opinion.

The Harses in the Born: The Cord/Card Merger

Phonetic symbols used in the section

[ɑ] as in *f**a**ther*
[o] as in *b**oa**t*

When I moved back to Utah after living in other states for fourteen years, I announced to friends and colleagues that I had found a home in Spanish Fork. "Spanish Fark, eh? I heard that the Marmons there worship the Lard. How harrible!" One of the mergers that has the most negative stigma attached to it is the *cord/card* merger. This happens when the vowel [o][66] before *r* sounds merges with [ɑ].[67] The merger results in a mostly identical pronunciation for pairs of words such as *born/barn*, *cord/card*, *four/far*, and *pour/par*. You are probably guessing, by now, that this merger is not unique to Utah, and you'd be right. It occurs in some dialects in England,[68] and I've personally observed it in Ireland, where the town of *Cork* is pronounced with an [a]. In the United States, the *cord/card* merger is concentrated in parts of Texas and in St. Louis.[69] The pronunciation of *Florida* in one survey[70] yielded many cases without [o] but resulted in other [a]-like vowels[71] scattered throughout the country, particularly in the Northeast and South.

The *Cord/Card* Merger: Previous Research

Pardoe[72] made the first scholarly reference to this merger in Utah in 1935. According to his personal observations, it was especially common in Utah and Sanpete Counties, and he attributed the merger to the influence of the immigrants from the Northeast. Many things argue for linguistic ties to the Northeast. Carr[73] and Carver[74] traced many vocabulary items used in Utah to that part of the country. This observation is supported by the fact that in 1880, 26 percent of the U.S.-born residents of Utah hailed from New York, Pennsylvania, or Massachusetts, and these settlers may have exerted a founder's effect on the newly developing dialect in Utah.[75]

Genetic testing has also confirmed the strong ties between Utah and the Northeast. One of the companies that promotes genetic testing, Ancestry, sorted through the DNA of its clients, grouped people with similar genetic characteristics together, and plotted them on a map.[76] In general, genetically similar people tend to live in the same geographical area. However, one of Ancestry's groups was widely separated. Their denomination for this group is called Northeast and Utah (figure 5.29). In a court of law, this kind of evidence would not constitute definitive proof, but even as circumstantial evidence it is worth consideration. Perhaps the Northeasterners brought the *cord/card* merger to Utah along with their genetic material.

The rise and fall of the *cord/card* merger has been well documented. By listening to recordings of Utahns born in the nineteenth century, Bowie[77] noticed that the merger became more prevalent in those born in the late 1800s. In 1969, Helquist[78] asked Utahns to read a passage containing these seven words: *form, horses, corn, born, horn, lord, cord*. Speakers in the oldest age group, comprised of those born between 1874 and 1920, merged [o] into [a] in about 80 percent of the cases. The merger was nearly complete for them. From that point on, however, the merger began to reverse. The younger

Figure 5.29. Northeast and Utah grouping of people with similar genetic characteristics according to Ancestry.com. (Credit: Original unmodified blank map of U.S. created by Kaboom88, public domain, https://commons.wikimedia.org/w/index.php?curid=2989307)

respondents born between 1921 and 1945 merged only about 70 percent of the time, and this number plummeted to about 30 percent for those born between 1946 and 1960. Lillie's youngest participants, who were born between 1967 and 1979, pronounced the vowels in *born* and *war* as [ɑ] in only 1 percent and 8.8 percent of the cases, respectively.[79]

One factor that surely influenced the fall of the *cord/card* merger is that it became stigmatized and associated more with the speech of older, less educated speakers[80] and with rural-dwelling speakers.[81] When variant pronunciations exist in a community and one of them is stigmatized, it is common for speakers to be self-conscious of their speech and to hypercorrect. That is, the speakers try to use the prestige form, but they use it in the wrong words. For example, since *barn* and *born* are often merged into *b[a]rn*, when a person misapplies [o] to the word *barn* yielding *b[o]rn*, that hypercorrection is evidence for the stigmatization of the *cord/card* merger. Both Helquist and Cook document hypercorrection in their studies.[82] The negative view toward the merger was revealed in a more recent matched guise study as well.[83] Speakers who merged were judged as less intelligent and less friendly. Other factors come into play in addition to age, rurality, and education. For example, women merge more than men do.[84] In 1997 the merger was also much greater in southern and central Utah compared to the northern third of the state.[85]

The *Cord/Card* Merger: Survey Results

The survey participants were presented with the four test questions in table 5.16, and 92 percent of the responses were matched with [o]. Only 8 percent indicated a merger because they were matched with [ɑ]. Nevertheless, a number of variables were significant (table 5.17), including the county the participants presently reside in. The post hoc analysis revealed that only a few comparisons between counties were significant; namely, there were fewer merged responses in Utah County when compared with Juab and Sanpete Counties. The difference between Juab and Salt Lake Counties approached significance.[86] Keep in mind that, in figure 5.30, the counties marked with asterisks had fewer than 10 responses, and in Morgan County, which came out on top numerically, there were only 20 responses, which makes it difficult to compare statistically to other counties. Juab and Sanpete, on the other hand, had 110 and 82 responses, respectively. Pardoe mentioned Sanpete and Utah as counties he felt merged more.[87]

Previous studies demonstrated that the merger was preferred less often by each successive generation. In contrast, the results of this survey indicate the opposite: the younger participants preferred the merger response more than the older participants did (figure 5.31), although the difference was small—10 percent to 6 percent. Given the negative associations the merger has, it would

Table 5.16. Test Questions and Responses for the *Cord/Card* Merger

Test Question for the Cord/Card Merger	Test Words and Responses
How do you pronounce the highlighted part of the word ___? Like the word ___.	**Co**rd
	A **co**n
	B **co**ne
	Lord
	A **la**wn
	B **lo**ne
	horse
	A **ho**p
	B **ho**pe
	be**fo**re
	A **faw**n
	B **pho**ne

Table 5.17. Statistical Results of the *Cord/Card* Merger

Predictor	χ^2	df	p	R^2
County of Residence	58.60	28	< .001	.437
Age	6.82	1	0.009	.007
Religion	8.45	3	0.038	.029
Education	11.06	1	< .001	.023

Marginal R^2 = .457
Conditional R^2 = .588

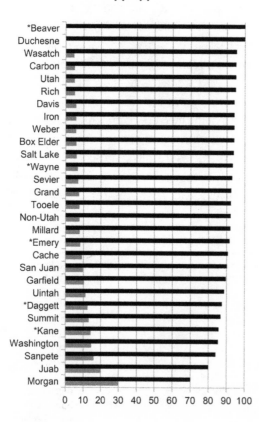

Figure 5.30. Percent of responses to the *cord/card* merger by county of residence.

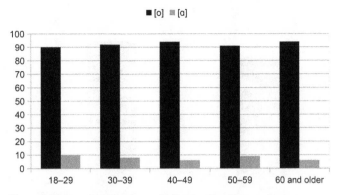

Figure 5.31. Percent of responses to the *cord/card* merger by age.

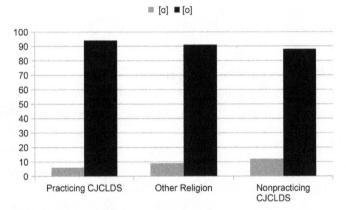

Figure 5.32. Percent of responses to the *cord/card* merger by religion.

be surprising to see it reversing and catching on among young Utahns. Could these results be an anomaly? What's going on in other states? Either way, further research into the phenomenon will provide the answer.

The influence of religion on this pronunciation surprised me. I fully expected the merger to be more advanced among members of the CJCLDS because it is the older pronunciation. Instead, the merger was less prevalent among practicing members of the CJCLDS (6 percent) than it was among members of other religions (12 percent), who merged slightly more often (figure 5.32). As far as education is concerned (figure 5.33), the merger is more prevalent among the less educated.

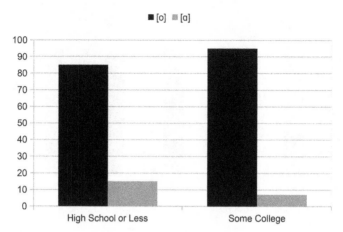

Figure 5.33. Percent of responses to the *cord/card* merger by education.

The *Cord/Card* Merger: Words Like *Laura*

Variant pronunciations of names such as *Laura* and *Lawrence* as *L[a]ra/L[o]ra* and *L[a]rence/L[o]rence* are fairly common, although I've never seen a systematic study of them. Words like these fit squarely into the *cord/card* merger, which is why I treat them here.[88] Three of the four test items I included in my survey (table 5.18) are proper names. The people who carry those names, and those who refer to people with those names, may have a set preference for the vowel in their names. This contrasts with variation in pronunciation of other kinds of words, such as the variant pronunciations of *working* versus *workin'*. Unlike the invariant way a person pronounces their own name, *working* and *workin'* may be found in the mouth of the same speaker, but in different social and linguistics contexts.

The most frequent words beginning with *laur-* or *lawr-* are proper names:[89] *Laura, Laurie, Laurent, Laurence, Lauren, Lawrie, Lawrence*. While *laurel* is not always a proper noun, it can be. I hypothesize that the *cord/card* merger originally resulted in an [a] vowel in the majority of these words. Of course, people still could, and do, choose to call themselves *L[o]ra* or *L[o]rence*, contra the merger. However, the merger made [a] the most common vowel. Because these words are proper nouns, the exact pronunciation was lexicalized by speakers. This rendered them more immune to change, so even while the *cord/card* merger was dying out, the [a] vowel in these names resisted shifting into [o]. Their pronunciation was fossilized in an older stage of the language. The instances of *Laurel* as a proper noun would follow this same trajectory,

Table 5.18. Test Questions and Responses to Words Like *Laura*

Test Question for Words Like Laura.	Test Words and Responses
How do you pronounce the highlighted part of the word ___? Like the word ___.	**Lau**ren A **law**n B **loa**n C If someone I know is named ___, I follow their pronunciation. **lau**rel A **loa**d B **lau**d **Lau**ra A **law**n B **loa**n C If someone I know is named ___, I follow their pronunciation. **Law**rence A **lo**p B **lo**pe C If someone I know is named ___, I follow their pronunciation.

Table 5.19. Statistical Results for the Pronunciation of Words Like *Laura*

Predictor	χ^2	df	*p*	R^2
Age	62.97	1	<.001	.068
Gender	7.95	1	0.005	.010
Religion	13.03	2	0.001	.014
County Raised In	77.76	30	<.001	.263

Marginal R^2 = .299
Conditional R^2 = .500

while the non-nominal cases of *laurel*, as well as the word *laureate*, would have followed suite by analogy to the other *laur-/lawr-* words that are proper nouns.

In the survey, participants saw only two of the test questions and matched the vowels in words such as *Laura* to [o] or [ɑ]. In cases where the word was a proper noun, participants were given a third choice: *If someone I know is named ___, I follow their pronunciation.* All responses of this sort were removed from consideration in the statistical analysis, after which 72 percent of the words matched to responses with [ɑ], and 28 percent to [o]. Four significant

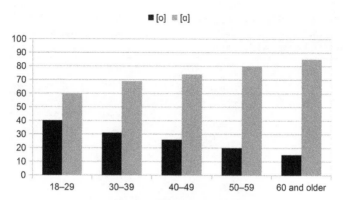

Figure 5.34. Percent of vowels matched to words like *Laura* by age.

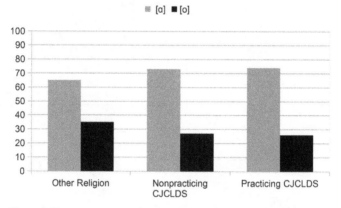

Figure 5.35. Percent of vowels matched to words like *Laura* by religion.

variables are related to the pronunciation of the names (table 5.19). The influence of age is quite robust (figure 5.34). Although the most common match was to [ɑ], it was much more frequent among the older speakers, while the younger the speaker was, the more [o] matches were chosen.

I think it is safe to assume that pronunciations such as L[ɑ]ra are older in Utah. They are more common among older speakers. The post hoc analysis on religion's influence on the pronunciations indicates that practicing members of the CJCLDS preferred them significantly more when compared to members of other religions (figure 5.35). This corroborates what Chatterton[90] observed in Cardston, Alberta, where members of the CJCLDS produced *Laura* with [ɑ] while nonmembers did not. Women also prefer the older pronunciation more than men (figure 5.36).

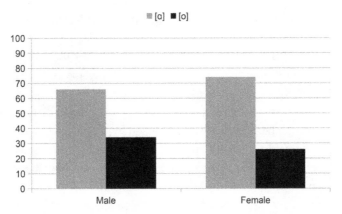

Figure 5.36. Percent of vowels matched to words like *Laura* by gender.

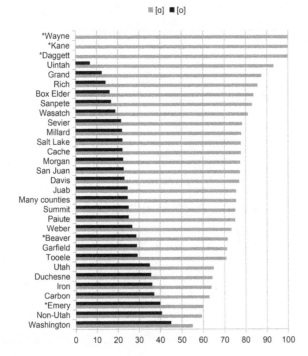

Figure 5.37. Percent of vowels matched to words like *Laura* by county raised in.

The region variable that gave the model the best fit was the county the participant was raised in (figure 5.37). Preference for [ɑ] ranges from 55 percent to 100 percent. Note that, in the table, countries with fewer than ten responses are marked with an asterisk. The county comparisons that the post hoc analysis flagged as significant were all contrasted with participants who were not raised in Utah. These results differed significantly from participants from Salt Lake, Davis, Sanpete, Cache, and Uintah[91] counties. The fact that Utahns raised outside of the state were more likely to prefer test words like *Laura* with [o] is also a sign that [ɑ] in these words is a characteristic of Utah speech.

In the survey results of the *cord/card* merger, only 8 percent of the responses indicated a merger because they were matched to [ɑ]. However, speakers preferred [ɑ] in words like *Laura* in 72 percent of the responses. I consider this further evidence of the fossilization of [ɑ] in these words. The alternation between [ɑ] and [o] in proper names may be explained by three things. The first is that even when the *cord/card* merger was at its apogee, there must have been some people who still held onto the older pronunciations of *L[o]ra* and *L[o]rence* in proper nouns. In other words, there has arguably always been some degree of variation. Second, in my experience, the [ɑ] pronunciations are stigmatized, just like they are in *Spanish F[a]rk* and *h[a]rrible [a]ranges*. That being the case, parents may have chosen to give their children unstigmatized names such as *L[o]ra and L[o]rence*. Third, immigrants to Utah from other parts of the country have brought *Lawrence, Laura, Lauren,* and *Laurel* with the [o] pronunciation with them, which has added to the variation in the pronunciation of these words.

OTHER VOWEL PHENOMENA

Sundee School: Pronunciation of *-Day* in the Days of the Week

Phonetic symbols used in this section

[eɪ] as in *l**ay***
[i] as in *L**ee***

Vaux and Golder[92] asked their online participants how they pronounced *-day* in the days of the week: *d[eɪ]* or *d[i]*. The participants could also indicate that they pronounced some days of the week differently, or that when the day of the week was an adjective, as in *Sunday school*, they gave it a different pronunciation than when it was a noun. All of these responses were scattered throughout the country, including in Utah where 5 percent of the respondents indicated that they pronounced them with [i]. Chatterton[93] noticed an age

Table 5.20. Test Questions and Responses to the Pronunciation of -day in the Days of the Week

Test Question for Words for the Pronunciation of -day in Days of the Week.	Test Words and Responses
How do you pronounce the highlighted part of the word ___? Like the word ___.	Mon**day** A **Da**mon B **de**mon Fri**day** A **Da**de B **dee**d Sun**day** A **dea**n B **Da**ne Satur**day** A **da**ze B **Dee**'s

difference among CJCLDS members and nonmembers in Cardston, Alberta, where older speakers pronounced the days of the week *d[i]* more than younger speakers did.

The questions in the present survey appear in table 5.20. Each participant responded to two of these questions, and the great majority of the test words were matched to responses containing [eɪ] (96 percent), while only 4 percent contained [i]. My personal observation was that older speakers favored [i] and younger speakers [eɪ]. I kind of fit between the two since the days of the week have [eɪ], but when they are adjectives, as in *Sunday school*, it's *Sund[i] school*. Nevertheless, the statistical analysis turned up nothing, not even age. Perhaps my observations were too limited, or maybe pronunciations such as *Frid[i]* have been so stigmatized that the participants provided what they perceived to be the correct pronunciation rather than their actual pronunciation. Once again, more research into this issue is warranted.

It's Been My Playsure: Pronunciation of Words Like *Measure*

Phonetic symbols used in this section

[ɛ] as in m**e**t

[eɪ] as in m**a**te

Table 5.21. Test Questions and Responses for the Pronunciation of Words Like *Measure*

Test Question for the Pronunciation of Words Like Measure	Test Words and Responses
How do you pronounce the highlighted part of the word ___? Like the word ___.	**mea**sure A **met** B **mat**e **trea**sure A **tre**ss B **tra**ce **plea**sure A **ple**d B **play**ed

Having grown up in the CJCLDS, when I was younger I was already accustomed to listening to the discourses of church leaders on television. When the leaders spoke of *treasures in heaven*, *earthly pleasures*, or *the measure of a man*, I was always struck by the way these septuagenarians and octogenarians pronounced the words *measure*, *pleasure*, and *treasure* as *-[eɪ]sure*, rather than what I generally heard as *-[ɛ]sure*. I just chalked it up as an old-man pronunciation. Savage,[94] for his part, found it to be associated with less friendly speakers.

Most dictionaries that provide pronunciations, whether they are American or British, give *-[ɛ]sure*. The one exception is Merriam-Webster, which gives both *m[eɪ]sure* and *m[ɛ]sure*.[95] Internet discussions of the topic point to the Midwest as the focal point of *-[eɪ]sure*, and many online discussions make it clear that people who use *-[eɪ]sure* are stigmatized or made fun of. I included three words in the survey to more closely examine this pronunciation in Utah (table 5.21), and all participants saw all three questions. The statistical results appear in table 5.22.

Table 5.22. Statistical Results for the Pronunciation of Words Like *Measure*

Predictors	χ^2	df	*p*	R^2
Age	51.8	1	< .001	.026
Region of Residence—Extended Wasatch Front	16.3	3	< .001	.008
Region Raised in—Extended Wasatch Front	13.5	2	0.001	.008

Marginal R^2 = .095
Conditional R^2 = .705

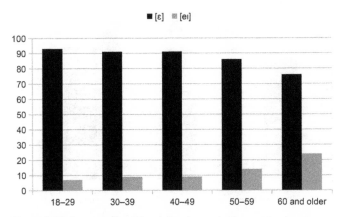

Figure 5.38. Percent of vowel matches to words like *measure* by age.

Only 11 percent of the responses were matched with [eɪ], while the majority were matched with [ɛ]. The conditional R^2 is much higher than the marginal, which shows a great deal of variation caused by individual differences between participants. The responses with [eɪ] ranged from 0 to 100 percent in the participants, and there were differences between the test words: [eɪ]: 16 percent *measure*, 9 percent *treasure*, 9 percent *pleasure*. Nevertheless, a number of predictors were significant. The results confirmed my experience that [eɪ] is used more often by older speakers (figure 5.38) and decreases with age. The region the participants were raised in and reside in made the same predictions, even though there is no collinearity between them. The vowel [eɪ] was more commonly chosen by participants who live outside of the extended Wasatch Front[96] when compared with those residing in the extended Wasatch Front, as well as when compared to those who weren't living in the state (figure 5.39). Once again, the use of [eɪ] is principally conserved by older speakers and rural participants.

The pronunciations of these words are related not only to the region the participants presently reside in but also to the region they were raised in (figure 5.40). There is no statistical difference between participants who were raised outside of the state, or who were raised in many counties, or who were raised in the extended Wasatch Front. However, participants who were raised outside of the extended Wasatch Front preferred the *m[eɪ]sure* type of pronunciation more than those who were raised within the extended Wasatch Front did. The fact that *-[eɪ]sure* is more frequent in older and rural speakers

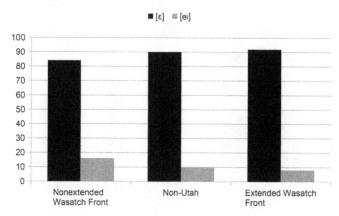

Figure 5.39. Percent of vowel matches to words like *measure* by region of residence.

suggests that it is the older pronunciation that has been largely replaced by -[ɛ]sure.

Odd Go if Ah Had Money: Variation between [aɪ] and [a] in Words Such as *Tie* and *I*

Phonetic symbols used in this section

[aɪ] as in *fight*
[a] as in *pie* (southern U.S. pronunciation)

Is Utah English influenced by southern dialects? Historically, the immigrants to the state did come from many parts of the country, the South included, but southerners were always a small minority. There is one trait that Utah may share with the South, however, which is the pronunciation of words such as *tie*, *pie*, and *I* as a single vowel [a] rather than as the diphthong [aɪ].

In his study of the recorded speech of Utahns born in the nineteenth century, Bowie[97] observed that 16 percent of the cases in which the diphthong [aɪ] was possible were pronounced as simple [a]. This became more common in the speech of those born later in that century. Beginning in the early twentieth century, the [a] pronunciation started its decline, according to Morkel's study.[98] She found the pronunciation to be more common in the Salt Lake Valley when

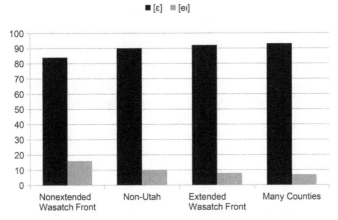

Figure 5.40. Percent of vowel matches to words like *measure* by region raised in.

compared to southern Utah, which in turn showed more evidence of it in its local speakers than in speakers from Utah and Cache Counties.

One difficulty with these studies is that the great majority of the cases consisted of the pronoun *I*, and contractions with that pronoun such as *I'd*, *I'll*, *I'm*. Of course, these are among the most frequent words with [aɪ]/[a], so by itself it's not surprising. However, the problem is that highly frequent words and expressions undergo phonetic reduction. For example, *I don't know* is often reduced to *I dunno* or even to something like *uh-ah-oh*. In like manner, the apparent shift from [aɪ] to [a] may actually be phonetic reduction, instead making *I'd go* sound more like *odd go*. In that case, [aɪ] to [a] is highly likely to be found in many English-speaking regions outside of Utah. Finding [aɪ] to [a] in less frequent words is better evidence that these cases involve a shift in pronunciation rather than phonetic reduction.

In any event, the existence of [a] instead of [aɪ] persists into the twenty-first century; Sykes documents it in the speech of seven residents of Salt Lake City,[99] in which the men produced more cases of [a] than the women did. There, it was not limited to *I* and its contractions. Sarver[100] examined the pronunciation of the word *tie* and found that 30 percent of all cases were [a], and for the participants aged fifty-five and older this rose to 60 percent. In another study of Utah County residents,[101] all cases of [aɪ] were found to be diphthongs. However, when the exact nature of the diphthongs was examined acoustically, the practicing members of the CJCLDS were seen to produce the glide of the diphthong (i.e., [ɪ] part) with the tongue raised significantly higher in the mouth than the nonpracticing members of the CJCLDS did.

To paint a fuller picture of how this pronunciation is related to Utah English, further research that includes a variety of words of different frequencies needs to be carried out. The speech also needs to be examined acoustically to determine if more fine-grained features of the vowels are related to social and linguistic factors.

There's Nothing Constant about Consonants

6

THE CHEERLEADER'S PALM-PALM: PRONOUNCED [l] IN WORDS LIKE *PALM* AND *CAULK*

Phonetic symbols used in this section

[l] as in *lead*

Discussions of grammar and pronunciations sometimes turn the most mild-mannered Dr. Jekyll into a ravenous Mr. Grammar Police Hyde. People generally assume that their pronunciation is correct and find arguments to support their assumption. For instance, some insist that the correct pronunciation of words like *palm*, *calm*, and *caulk* is to articulate the [l]. After all, the [l] is written in the word, right? However, when you scrutinize this evidence more closely you realize that *walk*, *talk*, *calf*, and *half* are also written with an [l], yet it is silent in those words. Once again, spelling doesn't help resolve the issue. People who don't pronounce the [l] justify it because it's not pronounced in words such as *walk*, *talk*, and *calf*, so in their view, people who do pronounce it in *palm*, *calm*, and the like are using an incorrect pronunciation.

As I've argued before, English spelling is far from precise. It doesn't indicate exactly how to pronounce a word but gives you only hints about the phonetic shape of English words. The silent letters in *island*, *debt*, and *salmon*, for example, were never pronounced. There was a time when people esteemed the art, drama, and language of the Romans to such a great degree that they figured English would be a much more elevated language if it were more like Latin. As a result, when the grammar mavens of the day encountered an English word that was similar to a Latin one (e.g., English *dette* and Latin *debitum*), they'd insert the letter from Latin into the English word (*dette* > *debt*), thereby exacerbating the messiness of the English spelling system.

Table 6.1. Test Questions and Responses for Pronounced [l] and Number of Questions Seen by Each Participant

Test Question	Test Items and Responses
Do you pronounce these words the same or different?	stalk stock
	com calm
	palm pom
	cock caulk
	A Same
	B Different

In any event, a written *l* may or may not be pronounced in English. I am unaware of any systematic study of pronounced [l] that ties the pronunciation to certain regions. In Utah, however, Savage[1] used a matched guise test to determine what pronunciations are associated with a speaker's perceived friendliness or intelligence. What emerged from the study is that pronounced [l] was not related to negative judgments of either trait, suggesting that there is no real bad vibe associated with it.

My survey presented the participants with two of the four test questions and asked them to determine if the pairs of words they saw were pronounced in the same way or in different ways. I assumed that anyone who chose *different* did so because of the lack of [l] in one of the words in the pair. There is an inherent problem with this assumption because it is plausible that someone pronounced both words without [l] but that the words have different vowels for that person. The most probable vowel difference is [ɑ] versus [ɔ], yet Utahns do not generally perceive these vowels as different (see the discussion of the *caught/cot* merger in chapter 5), so the influence of this confounding variable

Table 6.2. Statistical Analysis of Pronounced [l]

Predictor	χ^2	df	p	R^2
Education	4.20	1	0.041	.003
Age	67.70	1	< .001	.026
Religion	7.32	2	0.026	.004
Region of Residence—Extended Wasatch Front	16.71	2	< .001	.003

Marginal R^2 = .039
Conditional R^2 = .497

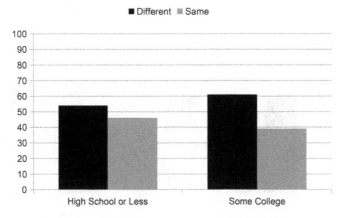

Figure 6.1. Percent of responses to pronounced [l] questions by education.

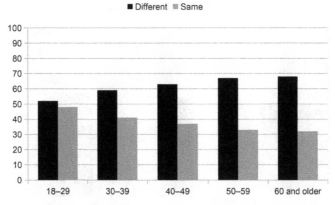

Figure 6.2. Percent of responses to pronounced [l] questions by age.

is probably minimal. In 60 percent of the responses, the pairs were judged as different, meaning that [l] was pronounced, while in 40 percent they were seen as the same. Table 6.2 shows the predictors that were significantly associated with pronounced [l].

Speakers with some college judged the words to be different; that is, they judged the words to have [l] in their pronunciation, more than those with less education did (figure 6.1). A distinct age difference was also present; younger speakers appeared to pronounce [l] in these words to a lesser extent than older speakers (figure 6.2). These two findings point to pronounced [l] as the

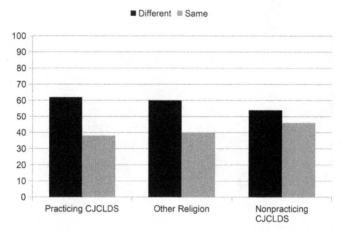

Figure 6.3. Percent of responses to pronounced [I] questions by religion.

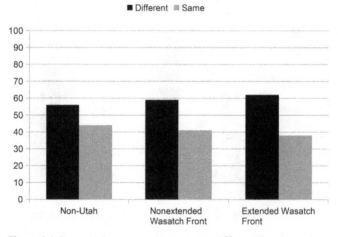

Figure 6.4. Percent of responses to pronounced [I] questions by region of residence.

older pronunciation. Both practicing members of the CJCLDS and members of other religions appear to pronounce [I] more often than nonpracticing CJCLDS members do (figure 6.3). The difference between other religions and nonpracticing CJCLDS approached significance ($p = .053$).

Small but significant differences were also observed depending on the participants' region of residence (figure 6.4). Participants residing in the extended Wasatch Front saw the words as being different in their pronunciation when compared with participants who don't presently reside in Utah and with those who live outside the extended Wasatch Front. Given these results, I predict that when pronounced [l] is compared with other states, Utah will have many words in which [l] is pronounced when compared to other parts of the country.

THE PRINTS OF WALES: INTRUSIVE [t] IN WORDS LIKE *ALSO*

Phonetic symbols used in this section

[t] as in **t**eam
[l] as in **l**ead
[p] as in **p**oem
[k] as in **c**orner
[s] as in **s**enate

When I hear people decrying the insertion of [t] into words as terrible English, I ask them why, and they invariably resort to spelling as their evidence: "It's incorrect to pronounce things that aren't in the spelling." If that is true, then it would also be incorrect to not pronounce letters in a word, right? That idea makes perfect sense to them until I point out words such as *castle* and *hasten*, in which [t] isn't pronounced. "Well, that's different," they respond.

When people hear an intrusive consonant in a word, they often assume that sloppy speakers just grab some random consonant and throw it in for no apparent reason. The truth is that intrusive consonants are never random; they are very predictable. There are many explanations for their existence,[2] but the basic idea is that the inserted consonant is one that naturally transitions from one sound to another. For example, the [t] in *also* (*al**t**so*) makes a nice transition from [l] to [s], something that a [p] or [k] wouldn't do. In the words *assumption* and *consumption*, which are related to *assume* and *consume*, not *assumpe* and *consumpe*, [p] is a transitional consonant that we write. Although we may pronounce *hamster* as *ham**p**ster*, we haven't gotten around to allowing the intrusive consonant into formal spelling yet.

Many other consonants serve this transitional role. The [k] in *streng**k**th* is an example. These transitional consonants do not just happen in contemporary English, either. If we went back in time we'd see *thimle*, *bramle*, and *pumkin*. Speakers inserted transitional consonants in these words so often that the new consonant came to be represented in the modern spelling: *thimble, bramble, pumpkin*. Unlike other inserted [t]s, the word-final [t] in *acrosst* can't be explained as transitioning between consonants. It's been around since at least the eighteenth century,[3] and is well-attested in on the East Coast.[4] It could be due to analogy with *crossed*.

In Stanley and Vanderniet's study,[5] six of their fourteen Utah participants produced a test word, at least once, with an intrusive [t]. This pronunciation is evidently stigmatized in the state, because Savage found that speakers who use it are perceived as less friendly.[6] I included nine test items in the present survey, and the participants were asked whether they pronounced each one with or without an intrusive [t] (table 6.3). Each participant saw *across*, four

Table 6.3. Test Questions and Responses for Intrusive [t]

Test Question	Test Items and Responses

Sometimes we pronounce letters that aren't written. For example, we add a **p** to hamster so it sounds like ham**p**ster. We also add a **k** to length so it sounds like len**k**th. Do you pronounce a **t** in the following words or not? How do you pronounce ___?	*celsius*
	    A *celsius*
	    B *cel**t**sius*
	Hansen
	    A *Hansen*
	    B *Han**t**sen*
	across
	    A *across**t***
	    B *across*
	false
	    A *fal**t**se*
	    B *false*
	censor
	    A *cen**t**sor*
	    B *censor*
	cancel
	    A *can**t**cel*
	    B *cancel*
	also
	    A *al**t**so*
	    B *also*
	else
	    A *el**t**se*
	    B *else*
	answer
	    A *an**t**swer*
	    B *answer*

Table 6.4. Statistical Analysis of Intrusive [t]

Predictor	χ^2	df	p	R^2
Age	6.43	1	.011	.002
Region Raised in—Extended Wasatch Front	26.02	3	< .001	.009

Marginal R^2 = .011
Conditional R^2 = .323

other test items, and one attention tester question. The two attention tester questions were *details/detailts* and *unsure/untsure*. Intrusive [t] is extremely odd in these words, and all data from participants who chose intrusive [t] in these words were eliminated.

Of the responses to these questions, 76 percent contained no intrusive [t], while 24 percent did have an inserted [t] in at least one of the test words. Age, and the region the participants were raised in, were significant variables. There is a very slight trend for younger speakers to use intrusive [t] more often (figure 6.5). When the regions the speakers were raised in were compared (table 6.4), the responses of those raised in many counties, outside of Utah, and in the extended Wasatch Front were statistically equivalent, and they all differed when compared to the responses of participants who were raised outside of the extended Wasatch Front. This result indicates that intrusive [t] is more common outside of the extended Wasatch Front. It's worth noting

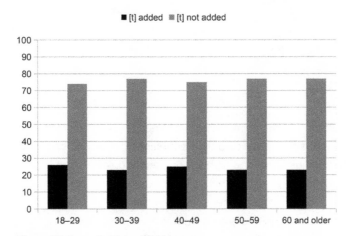

Figure 6.5. Percent of intrusive [t] by age.

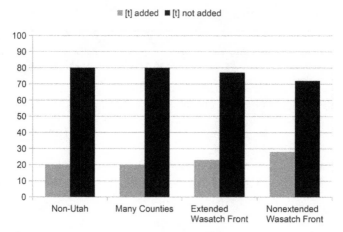

Figure 6.6. Percent of responses to intrusive [t] by region of residence.

that these two predictors account for only 1.1 percent of the variance, so these findings must be taken with caution.

THE ROCKY MOUN'UNS: ORAL RELEASE IN WORDS LIKE MOUNTAIN

Phonetic symbols used in this section

[n̩] as in butt**on** (syllabic)
[n] as in bu**n** (nonsyllabic)
[ʔ] as in foo**t**ball
[ɨ] as in ros**e**s
[ə] as in **a**bove

"Utahns say mountain weird." After I returned to Utah after a fourteen-year stint in five other states I heard this sentiment expressed quite often. It made one list of unique Utahisms.[7] When I pressed people on what they meant by that statement, they responded that Utahns drop the t in mountain. The idea of [t] dropping is far from accurate, and I shudder every time I hear it mentioned in the news. If the [t] were erased from mountain, the word would sound like moun, and it doesn't. What people are actually trying to express is that [t] has shifted its pronunciation in the word to a glottal stop, [ʔ]. Glottal stops are very common in American English. Try saying *Batman plays football.* Unless you are speaking extremely slowly or with a British twang, the sentence will come out as *Ba[ʔ]man plays foo[ʔ]ball.*

So, this pronunciation is not [t] dropping; it is glottalization of the [t], and it's not even unique to Utah. Throughout the United States, the standard pronunciation of *mountain* in casual speech is *moun[ʔņ]*, not *moun[tin]*. At least, that's how John Denver sang "Rocky Mountain High." What people have cued into about the pronunciation of *mountain* in Utah isn't really about the [t] at all; it's about what happens after the glottal stop pronunciation. After you pronounce the glottal stop, you need to release the air that you have blocked off. If you channel it through your nose, then the result is a nasal release, *moun[ʔņ]*; the glottal stop is followed immediately by a syllabic [ņ]. However, if you release the air through your mouth, then you produce a vowel before [n], resulting in *moun[ʔɨn]* or *moun[ʔən].* It is the oral release of the glottal stop that is associated with Utah speech, and you'll hear it in tons of words, such as *curtain, eaten, fountain, button,* and *Layton.*

The existence of the oral release in Utah has been documented. Eddington and Savage[8] asked Utahns to read a passage containing a number of words like *tighten* and *button,* and in 17 percent of the cases they registered an oral-release pronunciation. The highest use of oral releases was among young females who had spent most of their life in the state. In Stanley and Vanderniet's study of fourteen Utahns, it was exclusively the women who produced oral releases.[9]

The use of oral releases is often associated with Utah English and is usually described in pejorative terms, which has led the pronunciation to have a negative stigma attached to it. In a matched guise test, Savage[10] presented people with a series of audio recordings that were essentially identical except that in one case there was a word with an oral release and in another the word had a nasal release. The participants were asked to judge the speakers they heard on personality traits. Speakers whose recorded speech contained oral releases were judged to be less friendly and less educated than those who used nasal releases. The same result was obtained in a similar study carried out by Eddington and Brown.[11] In addition to the ratings of less friendly and less educated, this 2021 study found that speakers using oral releases were considered to be more rural. The Utahns who judged the speakers also felt that those using oral releases were more likely to be Utahns, rather than from another state.

While these studies correctly identify oral releases as a feature of many Utahns' speech, they do nothing to prove that oral releases are exclusively Utahn. After I presented a paper on oral releases in Utah at a linguistics conference, a number of fellow linguists approached me to tell me that they had observed this pronunciation in California, Vermont, and Connecticut. Others pointed me to internet discussions and parodies of the pronunciation in the speech of New Mexicans and Indianans. One researcher observed it in the speech of a New Yorker.[12] This experience prompted me to team up with my colleague Earl Brown to investigate the pronunciation outside of Utah.[13] Using a similar method to Eddington and Savage,[14] we extended the search to three other states and found oral releases in 24 percent of the instances of words like *mountain* and *button* in New Mexico, 12 percent in Utah, 9 percent in Indiana, and 2 percent in Mississippi. In sum, it is safe to conclude that oral releases are definitely a feature of Utah English but that they are not exclusive to the Beehive State.

Summary and Conclusions

7

I realize that I've covered a lot of factors and presented a dizzying amount of numbers in the previous chapters. In this section, my goal is to tie all of it together. I sought to answer a number of questions when I decided to write this book. First, how can we best divide the state into dialect regions? Second, what traits are dying out or gaining strength in the state? Third, how do these characteristics vary according to social variables such as gender, education, and religion? Fourth, what are the true and the supposed characteristics of Utah English?

DIVIDING UTAH INTO DIALECT REGIONS

Lillie[1] proposed that Utah can be divided into three dialect regions based on the northern, central, and southern thirds of the state. Along with her tripartite division, I contrasted the limited and extended Wasatch Front against the remainder of the state. Figure 7.1 summarizes how often each variable was significant in the analyses of the phenomena studied in the survey. Interactions between variables are not counted here. Figure 7.2 gives the average strength (R^2) each variable had in predicting the traits studied in the survey. Please note that in figure 7.2 the average R^2 of county raised in was actually .337, which is off the chart, but scaling the chart so high would make it difficult to perceive the differences between the other bars. Gray bars indicate the regional grouping based on the region the participants were raised in, while black designates the region the participants reside in. Finally, bars with diagonal stripes show other variables not related to regions.

In the statistical analyses, the northern, central, and southern division was significant in six analyses, with an average R^2 of .021. This division, while important, is overshadowed by the division of the state into the Wasatch Front

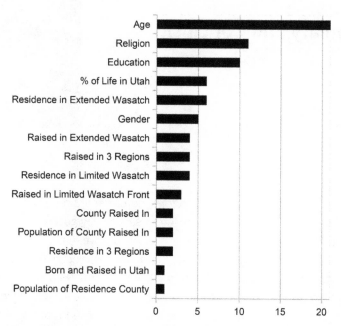

Figure 7.1. How often the variables were significant in the statistical analyses.

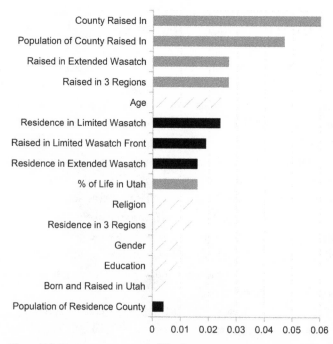

Figure 7.2. The average strength (R^2) of each variable in the analyses of the tested features.

versus non-Wasatch Front regions. The limited Wasatch Front was significant in seven analyses (eight if you include one interaction with age), with an average R^2 of .022, and the extended Wasatch Front was significant in ten analyses with an average R^2 of .022.

One problem with the proposed dialect areas is that both my dialect division and Lillie's were determined principally on a subjective basis. A more objective way of determining dialect boundaries is to allow a computational algorithm to draw the lines. To this end, the percentage of each survey item response was calculated for the county the participants were raised and the county they resided in. First, the counties were grouped into clusters of two, three, and four groups using a hierarchical clustering dendogram.[2] They were also grouped using a fuzzy C means algorithm[3] without specifying how many clusters to divide the data into. I took the resulting eight groupings and tabulated the number of times each county was paired with every other county then applied a fuzzy C clustering algorithm on the resulting table of county pairings. It yielded a division of the state into two dialect areas (figure 7.3) which doesn't correspond to either Lillie's or the dialect areas I originally proposed. One contiguous dialect group stretches from Cache County in the north to Juab County in the south, and this northern dialect region also takes in distant Iron and Washington Counties. I'll refer to these gray counties as urban and the white counties as rural.

Juab and Wasatch Counties are demographically rural but pattern with the urban counties linguistically. Including Juab County in the urban group makes sense considering half the residents of Juab County reside in Nephi, which is only a nineteen-mile freeway drive from Santaquin in Utah County. In like manner, the county seat of Wasatch County, Heber City, lies a mere twenty-eight miles from Utah County. The two urban southern counties that are geographically separated from the northern urban counties are Iron and Washington

Table 7.1. How the Three Regions Influenced Factors in the Survey

Factors	Raised or Reside	Three Regions Compared
To Stay or to Go (vs. *For Here or to Go*)	Raised and Reside	Northern > Central > Southern
You Bet Instead of *You're Welcome*	Raised	Central > Southern > Northern
Pronunciation of *Tour* with [o] Vowel	Raised	Central > Northern > Southern
Vowel [ʊ] in Words Like *Pull*	Raised	Southern > Northern > Central
Vowel [ʌ] in Words Like *Pull*	Reside	Northern > Southern > Central

Table 7.2. How Wasatch Front and Non-Wasatch Front Regions Influenced Factors in the Survey

Factors	Raised or Reside	Wasatch Front	Non-Wasatch Front
Help Who's/Whoever's Next	Raised	More *Help Whoever's Next*	More *Help Who's Next*
(Oh) For + Adjective	Raised and Reside	Less Accepted	More Accepted
Roof as r[ʊ]f[1]	Raised	Fewer [ʊ]	More [ʊ]
Name for Carbonated Drink (2 Analyses Combined)	Reside	More *Soda*	More *Pop*
Vowel in Words Like *Pool* (2 Analyses Combined)	Raised and Reside	More [u]	More [ʊ]
Vowel [ʊ] in Words Like *Pull*	Reside	More [ʊ]	More Other Vowel
Vowel in Words Like *Pen*	Raised and Reside	More [ɛ]	More [ɪ]
Vowel in Words Like *Measure*	Raised and Reside	More [ɛ]	More [eɪ]
Pronounced [l] in Words Like *Palm*	Reside	More [l]	Fewer [l]
Intrusive [t] in Words like *Else*	Raised	Fewer [t]	More [t]

Counties. In Iron County, 58 percent of the 55,000 Utahns who call it home live in Cedar City, a college town also located on Interstate 15, while Washington County houses the largest population outside of the Wasatch Front.

In the survey, the participants only indicated the county they belonged to, not the city, so it wasn't possible to subdivide counties. However, consider figure 7.4 which highlights in gray those areas of the state with a population of one hundred people per square mile or greater according to the 2010 United States Census. The most populated areas of Box Elder, Tooele, Juab, Wasatch, and Summit Counties are located closest to the Wasatch Front. This makes me suspect that there may be dialectal differences between the most and least populated parts of those counties. Perhaps this warrants narrowing the urban Utah dialect to the circled regions and expanding the rural dialect to areas outside the circled urban zones.

There are a number of possible reasons why urban and rural Utah speech is different. The Wasatch Front has experienced a much larger population growth compared to the rest of the state. The growth rate for the limited Wasatch Front in 2020 was 17.4 percent, and for the extended Wasatch Front 22.3 percent.[4] These numbers contrast with the 7.7 percent rate for areas outside of the Wasatch Front. In like manner, Washington County is one of the fastest growing counties in the country. It is safe to assume that much of the growth involves people moving to Utah from other states. Therefore, dialect mixing

Figure 7.3. Dialect groups according to hierarchical clustering dendogram algorithm.

in the more populated areas may have had the effect of tempering or diluting traditional Utah characteristics there when compared to the rest of the state.

In many cases, the responses of participants who were raised in or reside in the Wasatch Front ranked closer to those of participants who were either not raised in Utah or don't presently live in the state than they did with responses of Utahns who were raised or reside outside of the Wasatch Front (e.g., non-Utah > Wasatch Front > non-Wasatch Front). This is true in twelve of the sixteen analyses in which the region participants were raised in or the region of residence contrasted Wasatch Front and non-Wasatch Front participants. This means that the speech of those living in the Wasatch Front is less Utah-like than the speech of those living outside of the Wasatch Front.

WHERE IS UTAH ENGLISH HEADED? AGE-APPARENT EFFECTS

The majority of the survey data I've reported was collected by sampling Utahns at one point in time. This methodology doesn't allow us to make concrete

Figure 7.4. Population centers and dialect boundaries based on population density.

conclusions about what direction Utah English is taking over time. In a few cases, I've been able to compare my survey with older surveys to see how time has affected a particular phenomenon. I trust that twenty to thirty years from now someone will carry out another survey of these phenomena and use these results as a point of comparison so that we can gauge how Utah English has actually evolved with time.

There is, however, one way to extrapolate the influence of time from the cross-sectional survey data we have, and that is by examining the differences between the younger and older survey respondents. As I discussed previously, age was the predictor variable that was most often found to be significant in the analyses of the survey data, which provides us with a good deal of apparent-time influences. These are summarized in table 7.3. When younger participants chose a particular outcome significantly more often than older participants did, we can take that as evidence that a particular word, phrase, or pronunciation may be on its way in. The reverse tells us that the factor may be on its way out. The results in table 7.3 are based only on my survey, unless otherwise noted.

Table 7.3. Age-Apparent Trends

Word or Phenomenon	Age-Apparent Trend
For here or to go (vs. *To stay or to go*)	In
Mm-hmm or *uh huh* for *You're welcome*	In
You bet for *You're welcome*	In
(Oh) For + Adjective	Out
Propredicate *Do*	Out
Roof as r[ʊ]f	Out[a]
Carbonated Drink: *Soda*	In
Carbonated Drink: *Pop*	Out
Carbonated Drink: Other Terms besides *Soda* and *Pop*	Out
Tour as t[o]r	In
Route as a Verb as r[aʊ]te	Out
Words Like *Fail* with [ɛ] Vowel	(Lillie 1998, In; Sarver 2004, In)
Words Like *Feel* with [ɪ] Vowel	(Lillie 1998, In)
Words Like *Hull* with Vowel Other Than [ʌ]	In
Words Like *Pool* with Vowel Other Than [u]	In
Words Like *Pool* with [ʊ]	(Sarver 2004, In; Lillie 1998, Out)
Words Like *Pole* with Vowel Other Than [o]	In (Sarver 2004, In)
Words Like *Pull* with [ʊ] Vowel	Out
Words Like *Pull* with [u] Vowel	Out
Words Like *Pen* with [ɪ] Vowel	(Lillie 1998, Out)
Words Like *Beck* with [eɪ] Vowel	Out
Words Like *Cord* with [ɑ] Vowel	In? (Helquist 1970, Out; Lillie 1998 Out)
Words Like *Laura* with [o] Vowel	In
Words Like *Measure* with [eɪ] Vowel	Out
Words Like *Palm* with Pronounced [l]	Out
Words Like *Else* with Intrusive [t]: El*t*se	?
Words Like *Mountain* with Oral Release	(Eddington and Savage 2012, In; Eddington and Brown 2021, In)
Merger of [o] and [ɔ] in Words Like *Caught* and *Cot*	(Sarver 2004, Out)
Words Like *I'd* with [a] Vowel	(Morkel 2003, Out; Sarver 2004, Out)
Creek with [ɪ] Vowel	(Lillie 1998, Out)

[a]Age interacts with raised in limited Wasatch Front

 · What is most interesting in these findings is that they demonstrate that a number of the characteristics that are often associated with Utah speech are actually on the decline among younger speakers: r[ʊ]f, propredicate *do, pop, Oh for cute, to stay or to go, m[eɪ]sure, L[a]ra, pa[l]m, I'd* with [a], and cr[i]ck. Other

Table 7.4. Phenomena Influenced by Gender

Word or Phenomenon	Gender Trend
For here or to go (vs. *To Stay or to go*)	Female—More *for here or to go*
Oh) For + Adjective	Female—Less negative evaluations
Words Like *Hull* with Vowel Other Than [ʌ]	Female—Fewer [ʌ] vowels
Words Like *Pull* with [ʌ] Vowel	Female—More [ʌ] vowels
Words Like *Laura* with [o] Vowel	Female—Fewer [o] vowels
Words Like *Mountain* with Oral Release	Female—More oral releases (Eddington and Savage 2012)

proposed Utah traits are on the rise among younger Utahns: *t[o]r, moun[ʔɨ]n*, and most notably the numerous vowel changes before [l] that result in mergers between words such as *fill/feel, pull/pool*, and so on. These vowel mergers are among the most characteristics traits of English in Utah.

Previous studies documented fewer *cord/card* mergers among the young, while my survey indicates slightly more mergers in the younger speakers. Time will tell whether this finding is a fluke or an actual reversal toward more merg-ing of [o]r and [ɑ]r. Along the same lines, Sarver's data[5] suggest that the near merger between *caught* and *cot* in Utah County may be moving away from a merger. These are phenomena that need to be examined in more detail in future studies.

HOW DO GENDER AND EDUCATION INFLUENCE UTAH ENGLISH?

Before I carried out the survey, my instinct told me that gender would be a pervasive force in Utah English, but my instinct was mostly wrong. There are but few phenomena that split Utahns across gender (table 7.4). From the data I've compiled, it isn't possible to make a blanket statement about how gender is related to what factors are on their way in or out in Utah. On the one hand, women favor three things that are becoming more common in the state when judged according to the apparent-time influence of age: more preference for *for here or to go*, less use of the vowel [ʌ] in words like *hull*, and more use of oral releases in words like *mountain*. Men, for their part, are more on board

Table 7.5. Phenomena Influenced by Education

Word or Phenomenon	Education Trend
(Oh) For + Adjective	More education—More negative evaluations
Propredicate Do	More education—More negative evaluations
Carbonated Drink: Soda	More education—More soda
Carbonated Drink: Other Terms Besides Soda and Pop	More education—Fewer other terms
Words Like Pool with Vowel Other Than [u]	More education—More [u]
Words Like Pull with [u] Vowel	More education—Fewer [u]
Words Like Pen with [ɪ] Vowel	More education—Fewer [ɪ]
Words Like Cord with [ɑ] Vowel	More education—More [o]
Words Like Palm with Pronounced [l]	More education—More [l]

with the downhill demise of *(oh) for* + adjective expressions and the use of [ɑ] in words like *Laura*.

As far as educational level is concerned, participants who had some college education tend to be on board with most of the things that are on their way in. The two exceptions are that the more educated hold on to the [u] vowel in words such as *pool*, even though most of these vowels are in the process of merging with another vowel. The more educated participants are also more likely to pronounce the [l] in words such as *palm* even though that consonant is less often pronounced by younger speakers.

The college experience often involves interaction with people from outside one's own dialect area. This contact can make the student aware, either of the differences in their own speech patterns, or the fact that some characteristics of their speech are stigmatized. Furthermore, college students are more likely to be exposed to prescriptivist English teachers who espouse the idea that there is only one correct way to say something. This may be the reason that the more educated participants are less likely to prefer traditional Utah English traits in their own speech.

HOW DOES RELIGION INFLUENCE UTAH ENGLISH?

The work of Baker-Smemoe and Bowie[6] is groundbreaking because in it they document numerous cases in which religion is a factor in Utah English. The data from my study corroborates many of their findings and adds a number of phenomena in the state that vary depending on religion. We find these differences because religion markedly identifies certain social groups in the state. Practicing members of the CJCLDS not only fraternize during Sunday worship but also visit each other in their homes, unite for holiday activities, and work together on service projects. This socialization leads to a situation in which language changes, or the lack thereof, can be easily transmitted among group members. What's more, practicing members of the CJCLDS have a deep-rooted sense of community, and that manifests itself in their lifestyle and shared beliefs, as well as in their linguistic unity.

As a result, Utahns who are not members of the CJCLDS often feel excluded. They have less linguistic interaction with members, which apparently has helped them create their own group identity with its accompanying linguistic markers that often go in different directions than they do in the CJCLDS community. Many nonpracticing members were part of the CJCLDS community at some point in their life but no longer participate in the activities that serve to strengthen linguistic group identity. This is most evident in the analyses in which religion was a significant predictor. In eight of the eleven cases where the three groups are ranked with respect to each other, the linguistic behavior of the nonparticipating CJCLDS members falls between the participating members and people who belong to other religions. (Remember that other religion includes no religion as well.) In essence, the nonparticipating CJCLDS members may be seen as falling into the overlapping section of two circles in a Venn diagram when the circles represent the CJCLDS and non-CJCLDS communities.

The members of the CJCLDS, whether participating or not, hold on to a number of words and pronunciations that are more traditional in the state; namely, they use *pop*, pronounce *tour* with [o], and pronounce *route* as a verb with [aʊ] (table 7.6). Both CJCLDS groups use more nonstandard vowels in words like *hull*, *pool*, *bag*, and *Laura*, when compared with their non-CJCLDS counterparts. In like manner, the non-CJCLDS members pronounce words like *pen* with [ɪ] to a greater degree than do the CJCLDS members.

It is tempting to attribute the split between the areas that fall inside and outside of the Wasatch Front to religion. After all, Salt Lake County is the most populated county, and only 49 percent of its residents are members of the CJCLDS.[7] However, you need to consider that Utah County also belongs to the Wasatch Front. It is the second most populated county, and 82 percent of its residents are members. What's more, three counties outside of the Wasatch

Table 7.6. Phenomena Influenced by Religion

Word or Phenomenon	Religion Trend
Propredicate *Do*	Depends on percent of life in Utah
Carbonated Drink: *Soda*	*Soda:* Other > Nonpracticing CJCLDS > Practicing CJCLDS
Carbonated Drink: Other Terms Besides *Soda* and *Pop*	*Pop:* Practicing CJCLDS > Nonpracticing CJCLDS > Other
Tour as t[o]r	T[o]r: Nonpracticing CJCLDS > Practicing CJCLDS > Other
Route as a Verb as r[aʊ]te	[aʊ]: Practicing CJCLDS > Nonpracticing CJCLDS > Other
Words Like *Hull* with Vowel Other Than [ʌ]	[ʌ]: Other > Practicing CJCLDS > Nonpracticing CJCLDS
Words Like *Pool* with Vowel Other Than [u]	[u]: Practicing CJCLDS > Nonpracticing CJCLDS > Other
Words Like *Pool* with [ʊ] Vowel	[ʊ]: Other > Nonpracticing CJCLDS > Practicing CJCLDS
Words Like *Pen* with [ɪ] Vowel	[ɪ]: Other > Nonpracticing CJCLDS > Practicing CJCLDS
Words Like *Cord* with [ɑ] Vowel	[ɑ]: Nonpracticing CJCLDS > Other > Practicing CJCLDS
Merger of [o] and [ɔ] in Words Like *Caught* and *Cot*	Merged vowel is different between groups (Baker-Smemoe and Bowie 2015, Baker and Bowie 2010)
Bag raising: [æ] to [ɛ] or [eɪ]	More raising in CJCLDS (Baker and Bowie 2010)
Words Like *Laura* with [o] Vowel	[o]: Other > Nonpracticing CJCLDS > Practicing CJCLDS
Words Like *Palm* with Pronounced [l]	[l]: Practicing CJCLDS > Other > Nonpracticing CJCLDS

Front have a lower CJCLDS population than Salt Lake County's 49 percent: Carbon, San Juan, and Grand.

To put this information into better perspective, I calculated the percent of the population that belongs to the CJCLDS in each region.[8] The CJCLDS population in the limited Wasatch Front is 61 percent, and in the extended Wasatch Front it remains at 61 percent. That number rises only to 62 percent outside of the Wasatch Front. The takeaway is that varying degrees of CJCLDS membership can't account for language differences between the Wasatch Front and non-Wasatch Front regions of the state.

WHAT ARE THE CHARACTERISTICS OF UTAH ENGLISH?

The question of whether something is a trait particular to Utah does not have a black-and-white answer. In language, most everything is gradient, which leads me to give an answer with shades of gray. Let me begin with traits that, although they are found in the state, are so prevalent elsewhere that I just can't label them as Utah traits. Here I include the use of *biff*, the supposed Utah origin of *ride shotgun*, the pronunciation of *creek* and *roof* as cr[ɪ]ck and r[ʊ]f, and the rendering of *-day* in the days of the week as *-dee*. Like most westerners, Utahns can't perceive the difference between [ɑ] and [ɔ] in words such as *cot* and *caught*, although they may demonstrate subtle differences in pronunciation. Raising the vowels in words such as *bag* and *Beck* and pronouncing words like *pen* with an [ɪ] are also uncommon in the state, especially when compared with other parts of the country where these pronunciations often dominate. The *fill/fell* merger occasionally transforms the words *milk* and *pillow* into m[ɛ]lk and p[ɛ]llow, both in Utah and in the rest of the country. While the *pool/pole/pull* merger is widespread in the United States, in Utah, words with [ol], such as *pole*, are rarely produced with a vowel other than [o].

Another category could be called archaic Utah traits. These appear to have been common in the state at an earlier point in time but are less so in contemporary speech. The expressions *flipper crotch* and *fork*, meaning "valley" or "ravine," fit nicely here, as do *(oh) for* + adjective expressions. Often, archaic traits are retained only in the speech of the older generation of Utahns. Such is the case with the use of propredicate *do*, the *cord/card* merger, referring to carbonated beverages as *pop*, and pronouncing words like *measure* with an [eɪ] diphthong.

To classify something as a Utah trait, we need data from other states to compare the Utah data with. In many cases, there simply isn't data available that can be used to help classify a phenomenon as Utahn or not. So, another category would have to include phenomena that are common to the Beehive State, but that we don't know how Utah usage differs from that encountered in other states.

In this category I'd include the expressions *for here or to go*, *Mm-hmm* and *you bet* as alternatives to *you're welcome*, and *can I help who's next?* Others in this category deal with specific pronunciations: *tour* as t[o]r, words like *Laura* with [ɑ] instead of [o], pronouncing [l] in words like *palm* and *caulk*, and introducing [t] into words such as *altso* and *acrosst*. A number of mergers fit here

Table 7.7. Influence of the Percent of the Participant's Life Spent in Utah

Factor	Percent of Life Spent in Utah
To Stay or to Go (vs. *For Here or to Go*)	Higher Percent, More *To Stay or to Go*
Propredicate *Do*	Depends on religion
Carbonated Drink: *Soda* vs. *Pop*	Significant, but Nonlinear Relationship
Tour with [o] Vowel	Higher Percent, More *t[o]r*
Route as a Verb with [aʊ] Vowel	Higher Percent, More *r[aʊ]te*
Vowel in Words with [il] Like *Feel*	Higher Percent, More [I]

as well: the vowels in *fail* and *fell* merging into [ɛ], *fill/feel* into [ɪ], *pool* into [ʊ], *pull* into a vowel other than [ʊ], *hull* into a vowel other than [ʌ].

Although we don't have data from other states with which to compare Utah usages, there are a number of factors that were influenced by the percent of the participants' life spent in the state. This may provide a kind of indirect evidence that these factors are Utah traits (table 7.7).

Some traits don't lend themselves to easy categorization. Such is the case with the use of the vowel [a], rather than the diphthong [aɪ], in words such as *I* and *tie*. Numerically the entire southeastern United States outdoes Utah in the use of this pronunciation, which excludes it from the "common in Utah, not sure about where else" category. On the other hand, it's use in Utah has decreased over time, which could qualify it at an archaic Utah trait.

There are some characteristics that I don't hesitate to brand as Utahisms even though they are found in a few scattered areas outside of Utah. I do so because of their frequency in Utah English. The vocabulary items that belong in this category are *potato bug*, *water skeeter*, and *culinary water*. The stigmatized pronunciation that involves an oral release of a glottal stop in words such as *mountain* fits here as well. Is there anything truly unique in Utah English? The phrase *sluff school* comes close. It dominates Utah and southern Idaho but is found only sporadically outside this area. That leaves *scone*, meaning "fry bread," as the only word I will claim is truly unique to Utah.

WHERE DOES UTAH ENGLISH COME FROM?

Utah English has its origins in many different places, but the dialect of English that has most influenced the way English is spoken in the Beehive State is the speech of the United States. Yes, most of Utah's early settlers were from other areas of the United States, and Utah English is, and has always been, a variety of North American English. There are, however, distinct elements of Utah English that can be traced to other parts of the United States.

Many of the state's early settlers came from New England, and they brought with them a good measure of New England vocabulary.[9] I believe that the *cord/card* merger, which gave us *Spanish F**a**rk* and the like, is of New England origin. *Potato bug* is found in the areas of Upstate New York that many early Utah settlers hailed from.

Before being exiled from what was then the United States, many Utahns-to-be spent time in the midwestern states of Ohio, Illinois, and Missouri, and to a lesser extent Iowa. Bowie[10] claims that the origin of the Utah vowel system is the Midwest. *Potato bug*, while found in New York, is also the common term for this armored creature in northern Ohio, where the early members of the CJCLDS spent some time. Whether you can attribute the existence of these Utah characteristics to the Midwest is debatable, but Utah and the Midwest share *I'll help who's next*, and [eɪ] in words like *measure*.

The existence of the monophthong [a] rather than the diphthong [aɪ] in words such as *tie* and *I'll* is strongly reminiscent of that vowel in the southern United States. Of course, Utah did receive some southerners, such as the Mississippi Mormons,[11] who were among the first settlers to reach the Salt Lake Valley. Were their numbers sufficient to initiate a change in the pronunciation used by the state's nonsoutherners? Since the [a] pronunciation was also a feature of the Missouri dialect in the nineteenth century (think Tom Sawyer), perhaps it can be traced to there. Let me state, however, that I'm not a fan of this idea. Adopting a linguistic feature from another English variety requires lots of interaction and a sense of shared identity. The social situation at the time the members of the CJCLDS lived in Missouri was not one of mixing and integration, but of social and cultural isolationism, and downright intolerance by both sides.

As a result of missionary work by the CJCLDS, large numbers of foreigners packed up and left Europe for the desert valleys of Utah. We can probably attribute *for cute*, and like expressions, to the Danes. The massive influx of people from England may be responsible for the use of propredicate *do*, along with the terms *culinary water* and *scone*. The particular pronunciations of *tour* and *hurricane* may come from England as well.

Utah English is presently involved in many processes that are sweeping North America, such as vowel mergers before laterals (e.g., *pool/pull*, *feel/fill*, *hull/hole*). The *cot/caught* merger is the norm, not only in Utah but also in the entire western United States. Many supposedly unique Utah pronunciations of words such as *mountain, crick,* and *roof* are actually attested all across the country, and the use of *soda* appears to be encroaching from the West Coast and choking out *pop* in the state. In short, Utah English is principally a dialect of Western American English that has been shaped by the languages and dialects of the state's earliest English-speaking settlers and that is following the tides currently shaping the varieties of English spoken throughout the United States.

LIMITATIONS AND DIRECTIONS FOR FURTHER RESEARCH

Data gathered from an online survey do have some limitations. Unlike researchers who hold in-person interviews, the experimenter who conducts an online survey isn't present to answer questions or clarify what a particular test item is getting at. When a financial incentive is offered, which for my survey was $50 Amazon gift certificates, unscrupulous people may click through the survey as quickly as possible without giving thought to the questions, which produces worthless responses.

Even data from conscientious participants may be flawed. Often people believe they say one thing, when in actuality they say something else. Another issue is that the people who are most likely to participate in a study may not be representative of other people from the same region, or the same gender or educational level, and so on. In spite of these potential issues, online surveys have the advantage of being able to gather massive amounts of information in a short amount of time. A handful of bad answers are hopefully inconsequential given the large number of valid ones.

One concern I have already voiced is the small effect sizes, measured in R^2, that resulted in many of the analyses. Another issue is that the participants made categorical answers to questions of pronunciation, which is inherently continuous. Future research needs to involve recording Utahns as they are speaking in order to examine their pronunciations in much finer detail. Data that result from open-ended conversations tend to yield less-formal speech, hence more reliable data, when compared with data gathered from surveys such as this one.

Of course, no single study can examine everything that may be of interest in Utah English. I had to limit my study to avoid subjecting the participants to a

Table 7.8. Suggested Phenomena to Examine in Future Research

Pronunciation

Creaky voice
Intrusive glottal stops: co[ʔ]nference, cho[ʔ]colate
Both as bo**l**th
Thorough as thorou**l**
Root: [u] / [ʊ]
Wash vs. wa**r**sh*
Progr[æ]m / progr[ə]m
Coupon: [ku] / [kju]
Thanks, thank you: [ə]ank / [ð]ank
Crayon: many pronunciations*
-ing as *-ing[g]* or *-ing[k]*
-ing as [ən], [ɪn], [in]

Vocabulary

Dinner / supper
Sliver / splinter
Teeter-totter / see-saw
*It's (a) quarter to / of / till / before five**
Man-made body of water: *reservoir, lake, dam**
Pinky / little toe or *finger / pinky toe* or *finger*
*Downpour / cloudburst / other**
*Freeway / highway / interstate**
Anymore meaning *nowadays*
Based off of / based on
Elastic / rubber band
Babysit / tend the kids
Are you coming with? / Are you coming with us?
Pacifier / binky / others
Emergency brake / hand brake / parking brake / others
*Stop light / red light / traffic light / semaphore**
Bathroom / restroom / men's or *lady's room /* others
*Spigot / spicket/ tap / faucet**
*Earthworm / nightcrawler / angle worm**
*Frontage road / access road / other**
*Gas station / service station**
Store-bought / store-boughten

---

survey that would last hours and bore them to tears. In the course of preparing the survey, I found a myriad of other phenomena that need to be studied. I've placed them in table 7.8. Phenomena marked with an asterisk were dealt with in Lillie's survey.[12] I don't consider all of the phenomena in the table to be prevalent in Utah. Many of these items have already been investigated in other nationwide surveys. However, their status in Utah can be determined only in future studies. I trust that this list will encourage others to investigate the linguistic diversity that exists in Utah.

Notes

Introduction

1. David Crystal and Simeon Potter, "English Language," in *Encyclopedia Brittanica*, https://www.britannica.com/topic/English-language.
2. William Labov, "The Social Motivation of a Sound Change," *Word* 19, no. 3 (1963): 273–309.
3. See David Bowie and Wendy Morkel, "Desert Dialect (Utah)," in *American Voices: How Dialects Differ from Coast to Coast*, ed. W. Wolfram and B. Ward (Malden, MA: Blackwell Publishing, 2006), 144–48.
4. Wendy Baker and David Bowie, "Religious Affiliation as a Correlate of Linguistic Behavior," *University of Pennsylvania Working Papers in Linguistics* 15, no. 2 (2010): 2; Wendy Baker-Smemoe and David Bowie, "Linguistic Behavior and Religious Activity," *Language & Communication* 42 (2015): 116–24; Marianna Di Paolo, "Propredicate Do in the English of the Intermountain West," *American Speech* 68, no. 4 (1993): 339–56.
5. Benjamin Joseph Chatterton, "Religious Networks as a Sociolinguistic Factor: The Case of Cardston" (master's thesis, Brigham Young University, 2008); Marjory Ellen Meechan, "The Mormon Drawl: Religious Ethnicity and Phonological Variation in Southern Alberta" (PhD diss., University of Ottawa, 1999); Nicole Rosen and Crystal Scriver, "Vowel Patterning of Mormons in Southern Alberta, Canada," *Language and Communication* 42 (2015): 104–15.
6. Wendy Baker-Smemoe and Naomi Jones, "Religion on the Border: The Effect of Utah English on the English and Spanish in the Mexican Mormon Colonies," in *Language, Border, and Identity*, ed. D. Watt and C. Llamas (Edinburgh: Edinburgh University Press, 2014), 90–104.
7. Wendy Baker, David Eddington, and Lyndsey Nay, "Dialect Identification: The Effects of Region of Origin and Amount of Experience," *American Speech* 84, no. 1 (2009): 48–71.

Chapter 1

1. William Labov, Sharon Ash, and Charles Boberg, *The Atlas of North American English: Phonetics, Phonology and Sound Change* (New York: Walter de Gruyter, 2006).
2. Bert Vaux and Scott Golder, "The Harvard Dialect Survey" (Cambridge, MA: Harvard University Linguistics Department, 2003), http://dialect.redlog.net/.
3. Bert Vaux and Marius L. Jøhndal, Cambridge Online Survey of World Englishes, 2009, http://survey.johndal.com/results/.

4. Bert Vaux, "Dialects of American English Survey," 2018, https://www.dialectsofenglish.com/.
5. Stanley J. Cook, "Language Change and the Emergence of an Urban Dialect in Utah" (PhD diss., University of Utah, 1969); Di Paolo, "Propredicate Do"; Val J. Helquist, "A Study of One Phonological Variable in Urban and Rural Utah" (PhD diss., University of Utah, 1970); Larkin Hopkins Reeves, "Patterns of Vowel Production in Speakers of American English from the State of Utah" (master's thesis, Brigham Young University, 2009).
6. Daniel A. Sarver, "The Transferability of Utah English Characteristics: Second Dialect (D2) Acquisition in Utah" (honors thesis, Brigham Young University, 2004).
7. Diane DeFord Lillie, "The Utah Dialect Survey" (master's thesis, Brigham Young University, 1998).
8. I received permission to carry out this study from the Institutional Review Board at Brigham Young University, who deemed the project not likely to reveal the participants' personal information, nor to cause them emotional or bodily harm with the exception of possibly inducing boredom or eye strain.
9. "World Population Review," 2020, https://worldpopulationreview.com/us-counties/states/ut.
10. Baker-Smemoe and Jones, "Religion"; Baker and Bowie, "Religious Affiliation"; Baker-Smemoe and Bowie, "Linguistic Behavior"; Chatterton, "Religious Networks."
11. Following Lillie, "Utah Dialect."
12. The Jamovi Project, *Jamovi*, V. 1.2, Linux/Mac/Windows, 2020, https://www.jamovi.org/about.html.
13. R Core Team, R: A Language and Environment for Statistical Computing, V. 3.6, Linux/Mac/Windows, 2020.
14. Jacob Cohen, *Statistical Power Analysis for the Behavioral Sciences*, 2nd ed. (Hillsdale, NJ: Laurence Erlbaum Associates, 1988).

Chapter 2

1. R. J. DeBry and Associates, "These 11 Phrases Are a Dead Giveaway That You're from Utah," *Deseret News*, June 17, 2019; Emma Johnson, "Ten Words Only Utahns Use," *ABC 4*, April 26, 2021 https://www.abc4.com/news/everything-utah/10-words-only-uthans-use/ [sic].
2. Vaux, "American English."
3. Kurt Hanson, "20 Words You Need to Know How to Pronounce in Utah," *Daily Herald* (Provo, Utah), October 25, 2019.
4. Vaux and Golder, "Harvard."
5. Matt Canham, "Salt Lake County Is Now Minority Mormon, and the Impacts Are Far Reaching," *Salt Lake Tribune*, December 9, 2018.
6. *Online Slang Dictionary*, s.v. "lurpy," accessed December 16, 2020, http://onlineslangdictionary.com/meaning-definition-of/lurpy; *Rice University Neologisms Database*, s.v. "lurpy," accessed December 16, 2002, https://neologisms.rice.edu/index.php?a=term&d=1&t=4311.
7. Tim Wu, "What Ever Happened to Google Books?," *New Yorker*, September 11, 2015.
8. Herb Scribner, "Here Is Utah's Top Slang Word (Hint: It's Embarrassing)," *Deseret News*, June 27, 2018.

9. *Oxford English Dictionary*, s.v. "biff."

10. *Urban Dictionary*, s.v. "biff."

11. Mark Davies, The Corpus of Contemporary American English (COCA): 560 Million Words, 1990-present (2005), https://corpus.byu.edu/coca/.

12. Mark Davies, The TV Corpus: 325 Million Words, 1950–2018 (2019), https://corpus .byu.edu/tv/.

13. These examples are from Davies's TV Corpus: (1) "Saturday Night Live," 2016; (2) "Brooklyn Nine-Nine," 2016; (3) "Cougar Town," 2011; (4) "It's Always Sunny in Philadelphia," 2009; (5) "Ink Master," 2016.

14. DeBry, "11 Phrases."

15. Zöe Miller, "22 Phrases Americans Say That Leave Foreigners Completely Stumped," *Insider*, January 7, 2019, https://www.insider.com/confusing-things-americans-say -2018-4.

16. *Oxford English Dictionary*, s.v. "riding shotgun."

17. Mark Davies, Google Books Corpus (Based on Google Books n-grams), 2011–, http:// googlebooks.byu.edu/.

18. *Urban Dictionary*, s.v. "sluff."

19. *Dictionary of American Regional English*, s.v. "slough" (Cambridge, MA: Harvard University Press, 2013).

20. Mark Davies, The 14 Billion Word iWeb Corpus, 2018–, https://corpus.byu.edu/iWeb/.

21. These examples are from: (1) Provo Utah School District; (2) Brigham Young University, Idaho; (3) South Sanpete Utah County School District.

22. Example 4 from S. Worthen, *Oral History of Mildred Vercimak* (Lyman, Wyoming, 1989), accessed October 4, 2019, https://newspaperarchive.com/soda-springs-sun -sep-24-1953-p-2; example 5 from J. T. Saad, "Document Resume" (Boise, Idaho, 1972), accessed October 3, 2019, https://files.eric.ed.gov/fulltext/ED069030.pdf.

23. Elizabeth S. Bright, *A Word Geography of California and Nevada* (Berkeley: University of California Press, 1971).

24. Gardner R. Dozois, *Geodesic Dreams: The Best Short Fiction of Gardner Dozois* (Gordonsville, PA: St. Martins, 1992).

25. Vaux, "American English."

26. Bert Vaux (pers. comm.) indicated that the map for *sluff* he used in his survey was incorrect due to a computer glitch, and he furnished me with a corrected version that figure 2.2 is based on.

27. Vaux, "American English."

28. W. Bagley, *S. J. Hensley's Salt Lake Cutoff* (Salt Lake City: Oregon-California Trails Association, Utah Crossroads Chapter, 1992).

29. Vaux and Golder, "Harvard."

30. Vaux, "American English."

31. Bert Vaux and Marius L. Jøhndal, Cambridge Online Survey of World Englishes, 2009, http://survey.johndal.com/results/.

32. *Oxford English Dictionary*, s.v. "scone."

33. Vaux, "American English."

34. Lawrence Brown, "12 U.S. States with the Highest Concentration of English Ancestry," last modified February 20, 2014, http://www.lostinthepond.com/2014/02/12-us -states-with-highest-concentration.html.

35. Eric A. Eliason, "Utah Scones," in *This Is the Plate: Utah Food Traditions*, ed. Carol A. Edison, Eric A. Eliason, and Lynne S. McNeill (Salt Lake City: University of Utah Press, 2020), 52–55.

36. *Oxford English Dictionary*, s.v. "scone."

37. *Dictionary of American Regional English*, s.v. "flipper crotch."

38. Bright, "Word Geography," 91.

39. Sharon Wistisen, *A Funny Thing Happened on the Way to the Farm* (n.p.: Xlibris, 2010), 74.

40. Roger Ladd Memmott, *Heaven's Way* (n.p.: Gemstone Books, 2020), 30.

41. Afton Lovell (Pettegrew) Wilkins, *Warts and All: Family Memories* (n.p.: Xlibris, 2010), 74.

42. Kathryn Richards Sorenson, *Personal History of Kathryn Richards Sorensen, 1987*, accessed October 19, 2019, https://www.familysearch.org/service/records/storage/das-mem/patron/v2/TH-904-79685-1035-66/dist.txt?ctx=ArtCtxPublic.

43. *Dictionary of Regional American English*, s.v. "culinary."

44. Davies, iWeb.

45. Davies, COHA.

46. Davies, NOW.

47. Google Books Corpus, "culinary water."

48. Examples are from: (1) E. Hart, ed., *The Sanitary Record* (London: Smith, Elder, & Company, 1874), 1:229; (2) J. Phillips, *On the Drainage and Sewerage of Towns* (London: E & FN Spon., 1872), 22; (3) Thomas Carlyle, *History of Friedrich II of Prussia, Called Frederick the Great* (n.p.: Chapman & Hall, 1865), 5:114.

49. Davies, BNC-BYU.

50. Di Paolo, "Propredicate Do."

51. United States Geological Survey, s.v. "fork," accessed May 2, 2019. https://www.usgs.gov/search?keywords=fork.

52. Matt Stopera and Brian Galindo, "Do You Say These Things Like a Normal Person?" *Buzzfeed*, January 18, 2017, https://www.buzzfeed.com/mjs538/why-are-they-called-tennis-shoes-if-youre-not-even-playing-t.

53. Matt Aromando, "Where Would You Like to Eat?" August 6, 2015, http://www.mattaromando.com/tag/food/; "The Lingo," *Trip Advisor*, accessed October 29, 2019, https://www.tripadvisor.com/ShowTopic-g60763-i5-k5337859-o50-The_Lingo-New_York_City_New_York.html.

54. "Regional Vocabulary and Expressions within Québec," *Quebec Culture Blog*, February 3, 2015, https://quebeccultureblog.com/2015/02/03/regional-vocabulary-and-expressions-within-quebec-introduction-169/.

55. Hi Native, "Question about English (US)," January 19, 2015, https://hinative.com/en-US/questions/36072.

56. William Labov, *Principles of Linguistic Change*, vol. 2: *Social Factors* (Malden, MA: Blackwell Publishers Inc, 2001), 261–93.

57. There are no issues of multicollinearity between the region the participants were raised in and their region of residence.

58. David DeMille, "St. George, Utah, Is Nation's Fastest-Growing Metro Area, Census Says," *USA Today*, March 22, 2018.

59. X^2 (1) 104, p < .001, McFadden's R^2 = .104.

60. Lillie, "Utah Dialect."

61. Age: X^2 (1) 20.4, p < .001, McFadden's R^2 = .016; Region raised in—3 regions: X^2 (4) 19.8, p < .001, McFadden's R^2 = .016.

62. Geoffrey Pullum, "Can I Help Who's Next," *Language Log*, last modified December 4, 2005, http://itre.cis.upenn.edu/~myl/languagelog/archives/002690.html.

63. Lynne Murphy, "Can I Help Who's Next?" *Separated by a Common Language*, Oct. 19, 2007, https://separatedbyacommonlanguage.blogspot.com/2007/10/can-i-help -whos-next.html.

64. Pullum, "Who's Next."

65. Shakespeare, *Othello*, act 3, scene 3.

66. χ^2 (2) 9.71, p = .008, McFadden's R^2 = .004.

Chapter 3

1. *Dictionary of American Regional English*, s.v. "oh for" (Cambridge, MA: Harvard University Press, 2013).

2. Wishydig, "(Oh) for   !" Last updated June 26, 2009, https://wishydig.blogspot.com /2009/06/oh-for.html.

3. Janna Graham, "'Oh For' as a Scandinavian-Influenced Linguistic Feature of Minnesota and Utah," (Paper presented at the 60th Annual RMMLA Convention, Tucson, AZ, October 12–14, 2006).

4. Thanks to Wendy Baker-Smemoe for this insight.

5. Figure 1.2 in chapter 1 delineates the extended and limited Wasatch Front. Note that the extended Wasatch Front includes the limited Wasatch Front.

6. Mark Davies, "BYU-BNC," 2004, https://corpus.byu.edu/bnc/.

7. Led Zeppelin, "Babe I'm Gonna Leave You," on *Led Zeppelin*, released January 12, 1969.

8. Ronald R. Buttars, "Syntactic Change in British English Propredicates," *Journal of English Linguistics* 16, no. 1 (1983): 1–6; Kazuo Kato, and Ronald R. Butters, "American Instances of Propredicate Do," *Journal of English Linguistics* 20, no. 2 (1987): 212–16.

9. Hank Williams, "Why Don't You Love Me?" Side A, released 1950, MGM Records.

10. Ronald R. Buttars, "Cisatlantic Have Done." *American Speech* 64 (1989): 64–96.

11. Buttars, "Cisatlantic Have Done"; Peter Trudgill, ed., *Language in the British Isles* (Cambridge: Cambridge University Press, 1984).

12. Buttars, "Syntactic Change"; Martin Joos, *The English Verb: Form and Meaning* (Madison: University of Wisconsin Press, 1964).

13. Douglas Biber et al., *Longman Grammar of Spoken and Written English* (Harlow, UK: Pearson Education, 1999), 430–32.

14. Di Paolo, "Propredicate Do."

15. BBC, "Mormonism in the UK," Last updated October 6, 2009, https://www.bbc.co.uk /religion/religions/mormon/history/uk.shtm.

16. Richard L. Evans, *A Century of Mormonism in Great Britain* (Salt Lake City: Publishers Press, 1937).

17. BBC, "Mormonism."

18. Angela Brittingham and Patricia de la Cruz, *Ancestry: 2000*, vol. 3 (United States Department of Commerce, Economics and Statistics Administration: United States Census Bureau, 2004).

19. Di Paolo, "Propredicate Do."

20. Mark Davies, LDS General Conference Corpus, 2011, https://www.lds-general
    -conference.org/.
21. Trudgill, *Language*.
22. τ = -.222, *p* = .404.
23. Mark Davies, The Corpus of Historical American English (COHA): 400 Million
    Words, 1810–2009, 2010, https://corpus.byu.edu/coha/.
24. Kimberly Oger, "A Study of Non-Finite Forms of Anaphoric Do in the Spoken
    BNC," *Anglophonia, French Journal of English Linguistics* 28 (2019), https://journals
    .openedition.org/anglophonia/2936.
25. Davies, "BYU-BNC."
26. Di Paolo, "Propredicate Do."
27. These numbers were calculated from these data: https://en.wikipedia.org/wiki
    /The_Church_of_Jesus_Christ_of_Latter-day_Saints_membership_history; https://en
    .wikipedia.org/wiki/Demographics_of_Utah; https://population.us/id/; and data pro-
    vided from the Church History Department, via private email from Ryan Combs.
28. Buttars, "Syntactic Change."
29. Joos, *English Verb*.
30. Di Paolo, "Propredicate Do."
31. Lillie, "Utah Dialect."
32. Lillie, "Utah Dialect."
33. Di Paolo, "Propredicate Do."

Chapter 4

1. Mark Twain, *Adventures of Huckleberry Finn* (San Jose, CA: New Millenium Library,
   2001), 108.
2. Vaux and Golder, "Harvard Dialect."
3. *Merriam Webster*, s.v. "creek," accessed October 22, 2020, https://www.merriam
   -webster.com/dictionary/creek.
4. T. Earle Pardoe, "Some Studies of Rocky Mountain Dialects," *Quarterly Journal of
   Speech* 21, no. 3 (1935): 348-355.
5. Lillie, "Utah Dialect."
6. Vaux and Golder, "Harvard Dialect."
7. Vaux, "Dialects of American English."
8. When I included test item as a random factor, there was no difference in the conditional and marginal R^2 so I carried out a regression with no random factors.
9. Mark Abadi, "'Soda,' 'Pop,' or 'Coke': More than 400,000 Americans Weighed in,
   and a Map of Their Answers Is Exactly What You'd Expect," *Business Insider*, October 6, 2018, https://www.businessinsider.in/soda-pop-or-coke-more-than-400000
   -americans-weighed-in-and-a-map-of-their-answers-is-exactly-what-youd-expect
   /articleshow/66074186.cms.
10. Vaux and Golder, "Harvard Dialect."
11. Lillie, "Utah Dialect."
12. Baker and Bowie, "Religious Affiliation"; Baker-Smemoe and Bowie, "Linguistic
    Behavior"; Di Paolo, "Propredicate Do."
13. Lillie, "Utah Dialect."
14. Taken from Daughters of the Utah Pioneers historical marker dated September 25,
    1931, located at Heritage Park at 35 W. State Street, Hurricane, Utah.

15. *Cambridge Dictionary*, s.v. "hurricane," accessed October 26, 2020, https://dictionary
.cambridge.org/us/pronunciation/english/hurricane.

16. David DeMille, "St. George, Utah, Is Nation's Fastest-Growing Metro Area, Census
Says," *USA Today*, March 22, 2018, https://www.usatoday.com/story/news/nation
-now/2018/03/22/st-george-utah-nations-fastest-growing-metro-area-census-says
/448197002/.

17. Brown, "12 U.S. States."

18. Lillie, "Utah Dialect."

19. *Cambridge Dictionary*, s.v. "tour."

20. *Oxford Learner's Dictionaries*, s.v. "tour," accessed October 27, 2020, https://www
.oxfordlearnersdictionaries.com/us/definition/english/tour_1?q=tour.

21. Lillie, "Utah Dialect."

22. Vaux and Golder, "Harvard Dialect."

23. χ^2 (1) = 2.01, *p* = .045, McFadden's R2 = .002.

24. χ^2 (1) = -2.02, *p* = .043, McFadden's R2 = .002.

Chapter 5

1. Labov et al. 2006.

2. Eckert 2008.

3. Judges 12:5–6.

4. Raymond Hickey, "Mergers, Near-Mergers, and Phonological Interpretation," *New
Perspectives on English Historical Linguistics: Selected Papers from 12 ICEHL, Glasgow,
August 21–26, 2002. Volume 2: Lexis and Transmission* 252 (2004): 125.

5. Matthew Gordon, "The West and Midwest: Phonology," in *Varieties of English 2: The
Americas and the Caribbean*, ed. E. W. Schneider (Berlin: Mouton de Gruyter, 2008),
129–42; Labov et al., *Atlas*; J. Sledd, "A Canterbury Tell," *American Speech* 62 (1987):
185–86.

6. Marianna Di Paolo, "Hypercorrection in Response to the Apparent Merger of (ɔ) and
(ɑ) in Utah English," *Language and Communication* 12, nos. 3–4 (1992): 267–92; Alice
Faber and Marianna Di Paolo, "The Discriminability of Nearly Merged Sounds," *Language Variation and Change* 78 (1995): 35–78.

7. Labov et al., *Atlas*.

8. Penelope Eckert, "Where Do Ethnolects Stop?," *International Journal of Bilingualism* 12,
nos. 1–2 (2008): 25–42.

9. Sandra Clarke, Ford Elms, and Amani Youssef, "The Third Dialect of English: Some
Canadian Evidence," *Language Variation and Change* 7, no. 2 (1995): 209–28.

10. Lillie, "Utah Dialect."

11. Baker and Bowie, "Religious Affiliation"; Baker-Smemoe and Jones, "Religion"; Marianna Di Paolo and Alice Faber, "Phonation Differences and the Phonetic Content
of the Tense-lax Contrast in Utah English," *Language Variation and Change* 2, no. 2
(1990): 155–204; Lillie, "Utah Dialect"; Sarver, "Transferability."

12. Mark Davies, Corpus of Global Web-based English: 1.9 Billion Words from Speakers
in 20 Countries (GloWbE), 2013, https://corpus.byu.edu/glowbe/.

13. Labov et al., *Atlas*.

14. Lillie, "Utah Dialect."

15. Sarver, "Transferability."

16. Baker and Bowie, "Religious Affiliation."

17. Baker and Bowie, "Religious Affiliation."
18. Baker, Eddington, and Nay, "Dialect Identification."
19. Marc Giauque and Mary Richards, "Would-Be Robbers Walk Away Empty-Handed," *KSL.com*, April 11, 2008, https://www.ksl.com/article/3058039.
20. Di Paolo and Faber, "Phonation"; Lillie, "Utah Dialect"; Michèle Peterson, "Phonetic Variation and Change: An Analysis of Steel and Still," *Deseret Language and Linguistic Society Symposium* 14 (1988), 47–55.
21. Vaux and Golder, "Harvard Dialect."
22. Baker, Eddington, and Nay, "Dialect Identification."
23. Lillie, "Utah Dialect."
24. Labov et al., *Atlas*.
25. David Matthew Savage, "How We Feel about How We Talk: A Language Attitude Survey of Utah English," (master's thesis, Brigham Young University, 2014).
26. $X^2(1) = 4.58$, $p = .032$, marginal $R^2 = .002$, conditional $R^2 = .965$.
27. Conditional $R^2 = .965$, minus Marginal R^2 .002 = .963.
28. Lillie, "Utah Dialect."
29. Marginal $R^2 = .002$.
30. Conditional $R^2 = .965$.
31. Labov et al., *Atlas*.
32. Labov et al., *Atlas*.
33. Di Paolo and Faber, "Phonation"; Faber and Di Paolo, "Discriminability."
34. Lillie, "Utah Dialect."
35. Sarver, "Transferability."
36. Only 2 percent of the matches were with [o]. Baker and Bowie, "Religious Affiliation," found that words like *pool* were more often perceived as [o] by members of the CJCLDS.
37. Since four statistical analyses were run on the same data, a Bonferroni adjustment would lower the significant *p* value to .0125. This would render age as not significant.
38. Since four statistical analyses were run on the same data, a Bonferroni adjustment would lower the significant *p* value to .0125. This would render region of residence as not significant.
39. Sarver, "Transferability."
40. Lillie, "Utah Dialect."
41. I realize that this entailed matching [o] before a lateral, which is phonetically the vowel [ɔ] (e.g., g[ɔ]l) with [o] before a nonlateral consonant (e.g., bl[o]ke), but since [ɔ] and [o] aren't generally perceptually different in western American English, I don't consider it to be a confounding factor in the study.
42. $\chi^2 (1) = 9.61$, $p = .002$. Marginal $R^2 = .004$, Conditional $R^2 = .953$.
43. Sarver, "Transferability."
44. $p = .06$.
45. Baker and Bowie, "Religious Affiliation."
46. Labov et al., *Atlas*.
47. Lillie, "Utah Dialect."
48. Baker and Bowie, "Religious Affiliation."

49. Remember the extended Wasatch Front includes counties in the limited Wasatch Front.

50. Baker and Bowie, "Religious Affiliation."

51. Paul Kerswill, "Dialect Levelling and Geographical Diffusion in British English," *Social Dialectology: In Honour of Peter Trudgill* 223 (2003): 243.

52. Labov et al., *Atlas.*

53. David Bowie, "Early Trends in a Newly Developing Variety of English," *Dialectologia: Revista Electrònica* 8 (2012): 27–47.

54. Sarver, "Transferability."

55. Di Paolo, "Hypercorrection."

56. Baker-Smemoe and Bowie, "Linguistic Behavior."

57. Baker and Bowie, "Religious Affiliation."

58. Di Paolo, "Hypercorrection."

59. Joseph A. Stanley, "Are Beg and Bag-raising Distinct? Regional Patterns in Prevelar Raising in North American English" (paper presented at the American Dialect Society, New York, 2019).

60. Baker and Bowie, "Religious Affiliation."

61. Rosen and Scriver, "Vowel Patterning."

62. Vaux and Golder, "Harvard Dialect."

63. $\chi2$ (1) = 17.9, p < .001; Marginal R^2 = .012, conditional R^2 = .411.

64. Stanley, "Bag-raising."

65. Baker and Bowie, "Religious Affiliation"; Rosen and Scriver, "Vowel Patterning."

66. To simplify the discussion, I transcribe this vowel [o] rather than using the more precise symbol [ɔ].

67. The exact phonetic nature of the vowel resulting from the merger is discussed by David Bowie, "Acoustic Characteristics of Utah's CARD-CORD merger," *American Speech* 83, no. 1 (2008): 35–61, and Sarver, "Transferability." Joseph A. Stanley and Margaret E. L. Renwick, "Phonetic Shift /ɔr/ Phonemic Change? American English Mergers over 40 Years," Poster presented at *Laboratory Phonology 15*, Ithaca, New York, 2016, provide a study of how the vowels change in a single speaker's life.

68. John C. Wells, *Accents of English, Vol. 2: The British Isles* (Cambridge: Cambridge University Press, 1982).

69. Labov et al., *Atlas.*

70. Vaux and Golder, "Harvard Dialect."

71. [ɑ] and [ɒ].

72. Pardoe, "Some Studies."

73. Donna Humpherys Carr, "Reflections of Atlantic Coast Lexical Variations in Three Mormon Communities" (master's thesis, University of Utah, 1966).

74. Craig M. Carver, *American Regional Dialects: A Word Geography* (Ann Arbor: University of Michigan Press, 1987).

75. Bowie, "Early Development."

76. Anis Salvesen, "What 770,000 Tubes of Saliva Reveal About America," *Ancestry*, February 8, 2017, https://blogs.ancestry.com/cm/what-770000-tubes-of-saliva-reveal-about-america/.

77. Bowie, "Early Trends"; Bowie, "Early Development of the Western Vowel System in Utah," in *Speech in the Western States*, ed. V. Fridland et al. (Durham, NC: Duke University Press, 2017), 2:83–105.
78. Helquist, "A Study."
79. Lillie, "Utah Dialect."
80. Helquist, "A Study"; Cook, "Language Change."
81. Helquist, "A Study"; Cook, "Language Change"; Sarver, "Transferability."
82. Helquist, "A Study"; Cook, "Language Change."
83. Savage, "How We Feel."
84. Sarver, "Transferability."
85. Lillie, "Utah Dialect."
86. $p = .067$.
87. Pardoe, "Some Studies."
88. A reviewer raises the possibility that the merger in *born* is triggered by a tautosyllabic [r] which makes it different from words like *Laura* where the [r] belongs to the following syllable.
89. Davies, COCA.
90. Chatterton, "Religious Networks."
91. $p = .051$.
92. Vaux and Golder, "Harvard."
93. Chatterton, "Religious Networks."
94. Savage, "How We Feel."
95. *Merriam Webster*, s.v. "measure," accessed November 18, 2020, https://www.merriam-webster.com/dictionary/measure.
96. The extended Wasatch Front includes the limited Wasatch Front.
97. Bowie, "Early Trends."
98. Wendy McCollum Morkel, "Tracing a Sound Pattern: Ay Monophthongization in Utah English," (master's thesis, Brigham Young University, 2003).
99. Robert D. Sykes, "A Sociophonetic Study of (aɪ) in Utah English" (master's thesis, University of Utah, 2010).
100. Sarver, "Transferability."
101. Baker-Smemoe and Bowie, "Linguistic Behavior."

Chapter 6
1. Savage, "How We Feel."
2. Barbara Blankenship, "What TIMIT Can Tell Us About Epenthesis," *UCLA Working Papers in Phonetics* 81 (1992): 17–25.
3. *Oxford English Dictionary*, s.v. "acrost," accessed February 1, 2021. https://www-oed-com.erl.lib.byu.edu/view/Entry/1866?redirectedFrom=acrost#eid.
4. Language Log, "Acrosst," July 28, 2010, https://languagelog.ldc.upenn.edu/nll/?p=2495.
5. Joseph A. Stanley and Kyle Vanderniet, "Consonantal Variation in Utah English: What El[t]se Is Happening[k]?" (Paper presented at the 4th Annual Linguistics Conference, University of Georgia, Athens, Georgia, 2019).
6. Savage, "How We Feel."
7. Johnson, "10 Words."

8. David Eddington and Matthew Savage, "Where Are the Moun[ʔə]ns in Utah?" *American Speech* 87 (2012): 336–49.

9. Stanley and Vanderniet, "Consonantal."

10. Savage, "How We Feel."

11. David Eddington, David Ellingson, and Earl Kjar Brown, "A Production and Perception Study of /t/ Glottalization and Oral Releases Following Glottals in the United States," *American Speech* 96, no. 1 (2021): 78–104.

12. Lisa Davidson, Shmico Orosco, and Sheng-Fu Wang, "The Link between Syllabic Nasals and Glottal Stops in American English," *Laboratory Phonology: Journal of the Association for Laboratory Phonology* 12, no. 1 (2021).

13. Eddington, Ellingson, and Brown, "Production and Perception."

14. Eddington and Savage, "Where Are the Moun[ʔə]ns?"

Chapter 7

1. Lillie, "Utah Dialect."

2. Seol's algorithm (Hyunsoo Seol, SnowCluster: Cluster Analysis [jamovi module], 2020, https://github.com.hyunsooseol/snowCluster) was applied to the data in jamovi statistical software (the jamovi project) using the Canberra distance measure and the Ward D2 clustering method.

3. J. C. Bezdek, R. Ehrlich, and W. Full, "FCM: The Fuzzy C-Means Clustering Algorithm," *Computers & Geosciences* 10, nos. 2–3 (1984): 191–203, carried out in JASP (JASP).

4. World Population Review, 2020.

5. Sarver, "Transferability."

6. Baker-Smemoe and Bowie, "Linguistic Behavior."

7. Canham, "Salt Lake County."

8. My data comes from Canham, "Salt Lake County," and World Population Review, 2020.

9. Carver, *American Regional*; Pardoe, "Some Studies."

10. David Bowie, "Early Development of the Card-Cord Merger in Utah," *American Speech* 78, no. 1 (2003): 31–51.

11. Leonard J. Arrington, "Mississippi Mormons," *Ensign* (June 1977): 46–51.

12. Lillie, "Utah Dialect."

Bibliography

Abadi, Mark. "'Soda,' 'Pop,' or 'Coke': More than 400,000 Americans Weighed in, and a Map of Their Answers Is Exactly What You'd Expect." *Business Insider*, October 6, 2018. https://www.businessinsider.in/soda-pop-or-coke-more-than-400000-americans-weighed-in-and-a-map-of-their-answers-is-exactly-what-youd-expect/articleshow/66074186.cms.

Aromando, Matt. "Where Would You Like to Eat?" Blog. August 6, 2015. http://www.mattaromando.com/tag/food/.

Arrington, Leonard J. "Mississippi Mormons." *Ensign* (June 1977): 46–51.

Bagley, W. *S. J. Hensley's Salt Lake Cutoff*. Salt Lake City: Oregon-California Trails Association, Utah Crossroads Chapter, 1992.

Baker, Wendy, and David Bowie. "Religious Affiliation as a Correlate of Linguistic Behavior." *University of Pennsylvania Working Papers in Linguistics* 15, no. 2 (2010): 2.

Baker, Wendy, David Eddington, and Lyndsey Nay. "Dialect Identification: The Effects of Region of Origin and Amount of Experience." *American Speech* 84, no. 1 (2009): 48–71.

Baker-Smemoe, Wendy, and David Bowie. "Linguistic Behavior and Religious Activity." *Language & Communication* 42 (2015): 116–24.

Baker-Smemoe, Wendy, and Naomi Jones. "Religion on the Border: The Effect of Utah English on the English and Spanish in the Mexican Mormon Colonies." In *Language, Border, and Identity*, ed. D. Watt and C. Llamas, 90–104. Edinburgh: Edinburgh University Press, 2014.

BBC. "Mormon Emigration from Sheffield." *Legacies: UK History Local to You*. http://www.bbc.co.uk/legacies/immig_emig/england/south_yorkshire/article_3.shtml.

BBC. "Mormonism in the UK." Last updated October 6, 2009, https://www.bbc.co.uk/religion/religions/mormon/history/uk.shtml.

Bezdek, J. C., R. Ehrlich, and W. Full. "FCM: The Fuzzy C-Means Clustering Algorithm." *Computers & Geosciences* 10, nos. 2–3 (1984): 191–203.

Biber, Douglas, et al. *Longman Grammar of Spoken and Written English*. Harlow, UK: Pearson Education, 1999.

Blankenship, Barbara. "What TIMIT Can Tell Us About Epenthesis." *UCLA Working Papers in Phonetics* 81 (1992): 17–25.

Bolton, Herbert E. *Pageant in the Wilderness: The Story of the Escalante Expedition to the Interior Basin, 1776. Including the Diary and Itinerary of Father Escalante*. Salt Lake City: Utah Historical Society, 1950.

Bowie, David. "Acoustic Characteristics of Utah's CARD-CORD Merger." *American Speech* 83, no. 1 (2008): 35–61.

Bowie, David. "Early Development of the Card-Cord Merger in Utah." *American Speech* 78, no. 1 (2003): 31–51.

Bowie, David. "Early Development of the Western Vowel System in Utah." In *Speech in the Western States*. Vol. 2, ed. V. Fridland et al., 83–105. Durham, NC: Duke University Press, 2017.

Bowie, David. "Early Trends in a Newly Developing Variety of English." *Dialectologia: Revista Electrònica* 8 (2012): 27–47.

Bowie, David, and Wendy Morkel. "Desert Dialect (Utah)." In *American Voices: How Dialects Differ from Coast to Coast*, ed. W. Wolfram and B. Ward, 144–48. Malden, MA: Blackwell Publishing, 2006.

Bright, Elizabeth S. *A Word Geography of California and Nevada*. Berkeley: University of California Press, 1971.

Brittingham, Angela, and Patricia de la Cruz. *Ancestry: 2000*. Vol. 3. United States Department of Commerce, Economics and Statistics Administration: United States Census Bureau, 2004.

Brown, Lawrence. "12 U.S. States with the Highest Concentration of English Ancestry." Last modified February 20, 2014. http://www.lostinthepond.com/2014/02/12-us-states-with-highest-concentration.html.

Buttars, Ronald R. "Cisatlantic Have Done." *American Speech* 64 (1989): 64–96.

Buttars, Ronald R. "Syntactic Change in British English Propredicates." *Journal of English Linguistics* 16, no. 1 (1983): 1–6.

Cambridge Dictionary. Online at https://dictionary.cambridge.org/us.

Carlyle, Thomas. *History of Friedrich II of Prussia, Called Frederick the Great*. Vol. 5. N.p.: Chapman & Hall, 1865.

Carr, Donna Humpherys. "Reflections of Atlantic Coast Lexical Variations in Three Mormon Communities." Master's thesis, University of Utah, 1966.

Carver, Craig M. *American Regional Dialects: A Word Geography*. Ann Arbor: University of Michigan Press, 1987.

Chatterton, Benjamin Joseph. "Religious Networks as a Sociolinguistic Factor: The Case of Cardston." Master's thesis, Brigham Young University, 2008.

Clarke, Sandra, Ford Elms, and Amani Youssef. "The Third Dialect of English: Some Canadian Evidence." *Language Variation and Change* 7, no. 2 (1995): 209–28.

Cohen, Jacob. *Statistical Power Analysis for the Behavioral Sciences*. 2nd ed. Hillsdale, NJ: Laurence Erlbaum Associates, 1988.

Cook, Stanley J. "Language Change and the Emergence of an Urban Dialect in Utah." PhD diss., University of Utah, 1969.

Crystal, David, and Simeon Potter. *Encyclopedia Brittanica*. s.v. "English Language." https://www.britannica.com/topic/English-language.

Davidson, Lisa, Shmico Orosco, and Sheng-Fu Wang. "The Link between Syllabic Nasals and Glottal Stops in American English." *Laboratory Phonology: Journal of the Association for Laboratory Phonology* 12, no. 1 (2021).

Davies, Mark. The 14 Billion Word iWeb Corpus. 2018–. https://corpus.byu.edu/iWeb/.

Davies, Mark. "BYU-BNC." 2004. https://corpus.byu.edu/bnc/.

Davies, Mark. The Corpus of Contemporary American English (COCA): 560 Million Words, 1990–present. 2005. https://corpus.byu.edu/coca/.

Davies, Mark. Corpus of Global Web-based English: 1.9 Billion Words from Speakers in 20 Countries (GloWbE). 2013. https://corpus.byu.edu/glowbe/.

Davies, Mark. The Corpus of Historical American English (COHA): 400 Million Words, 1810–2009. 2010. https://corpus.byu.edu/coha/.

Davies, Mark. Google Books Corpus. (Based on Google Books n-grams.) 2011–. http://googlebooks.byu.edu/.

Davies, Mark. LDS General Conference Corpus. 2011. https://www.lds-general-conference.org/.

Davies, Mark. The Movie Corpus: 200 Million Words, 1930–2018. 2019–. https://corpus.byu.edu/movies/.

Davies, Mark. The TV Corpus: 325 Million Words, 1950–2018. 2019. https://corpus.byu.edu/tv/.

DeMille, Janice Force. *Portraits of the Hurricane Pioneers*. N.p.: Homestead Publishers, 1976.

Dictionary of American Regional English. Cambridge, MA: Harvard University Press, 2013.

Di Paolo, Marianna. "Hypercorrection in Response to the Apparent Merger of (ɔ) and (ɑ) in Utah English." *Language and Communication* 12, nos. 3–4 (1992): 267–92.

Di Paolo, Marianna. "Propredicate Do in the English of the Intermountain West." *American Speech* 68, no. 4 (1993): 339–56.

Di Paolo, Marianna, and Alice Faber. "Phonation Differences and the Phonetic Content of the Tense-lax Contrast in Utah English." *Language Variation and Change* 2, no. 2 (1990): 155–204.

Dozois, Gardner R. *Geodesic Dreams: The Best Short Fiction of Gardner Dozois*. Gordonsville, PA: St. Martins, 1992.

Eckert, Penelope. "Where Do Ethnolects Stop?" *International Journal of Bilingualism* 12, nos. 1–2 (2008): 25–42.

Eddington, David, and Matthew Savage. 2012. "Where Are the Moun[ʔə]ns in Utah?" *American Speech* 87 (2012): 336–49.

Eddington, David Ellingson, and Earl Kjar Brown. "A Production and Perception Study of /t/ Glottalization and Oral Releases Following Glottals in the United States." *American Speech* 96, no. 1 (2021): 78–104.

Eliason, Eric A. "Utah Scones." In *This Is the Plate: Utah Food Traditions*, edited by Carol A. Edison, Eric A. Eliason, and Lynne S. McNeill, 52–55. Salt Lake City: University of Utah Press, 2020.

Evans, Richard L. *A Century of Mormonism in Great Britain*. Salt Lake City: Publishers Press, 1937.

Faber, Alice, and Marianna Di Paolo. "The Discriminability of Nearly Merged Sounds." *Language Variation and Change* 78 (1995): 35–78.

Giauque, Marc, and Mary Richards. "Would-Be Robbers Walk Away Empty-Handed," *KSL.com*, April 11, 2008. https://www.ksl.com/article/3058039.

Google Books Corpus. s.v. "Culinary water." https://www.english-corpora.org/googlebooks/#.

Gordon, Matthew. "The West and Midwest: Phonology." In *Varieties of English 2: The Americas and the Caribbean*, ed. E. W. Schneider, 129–42. Berlin: Mouton de Gruyter, 2008.

Graham, Janna. "'Oh For' as a Scandinavian-Iinfluenced Linguistic Feature of Minnesota and Utah." Paper presented at the 60th Annual RMMLA Convention, Tucson, AZ, October 12–14, 2006.

Hart, E., ed. *The Sanitary Record*. Vol. 1. London: Smith, Elder, & Company, 1874.

Helquist, Val J. "A Study of One Phonological Variable in Urban and Rural Utah." PhD diss., University of Utah, 1970.

Hickey, Raymond. "Mergers, Near-Mergers, and Phonological Interpretation." *New Perspectives on English Historical Linguistics: Selected Papers from 12 ICEHL, Glasgow, August 21–26, 2002. Volume 2: Lexis and Transmission* 252 (2004): 125.

Hi Native. "Question about English (US)." January 19, 2015. https://hinative.com/en-US/questions/36072.

Jamovi Project. *Jamovi*. V. 1.2. Linux/Mac/Windows. 2020. https://www.jamovi.org/about.html.

JASP Team. JASP. V. 0.16.01. 2022. https://jasp-stats.org/.

Johnson, Emma. "Ten Words Only Utahns Use," *ABC 4*, April 26, 2021. https://www.abc4.com/news/everything-utah/10-words-only-uthans-use/ [sic].

Joos, Martin. *The English Verb: Form and Meaning*. Madison: University of Wisconsin Press, 1964.

Kato, Kazuo, and Ronald R. Butters. "American Instances of Propredicate Do." *Journal of English Linguistics* 20, no. 2 (1987): 212–16.

Kerswill, Paul. "Dialect Levelling and Geographical Diffusion in British English." *Social Dialectology: In Honour of Peter Trudgill* 223 (2003): 243.

Labov, William. *Principles of Linguistic Change*, Vol. 2: *Social Factors*, 261–93. Malden, MA: Blackwell Publishers Inc., 2001.

Labov, William. "The Social Motivation of a Sound Change." *Word* 19, no. 3 (1963): 273–309.

Labov, William, Sharon Ash, and Charles Boberg. *The Atlas of North American English: Phonetics, Phonology and Sound Change*. Berlin: Walter de Gruyter, 2006.

Labov, William, Malcah Yaeger, and Richard Steiner. *A Quantitative Study of Sound Change in Progress*. Philadelphia: U.S. Regional Survey, 1972.

Language Log. "Acrosst." July 28, 2010. https://languagelog.ldc.upenn.edu/nll/?p=2495.

Led Zeppelin. "Babe I'm Gonna Leave You." Track 2 on *Led Zeppelin*. Atlantic Records, 1969.

Lillie, Diane DeFord. "The Utah Dialect Survey." Master's thesis, Brigham Young University, 1998.

"The Lingo." 2012. *Trip Advisor*. https://www.tripadvisor.com/ShowTopic-g60763-i5-k5337859-o50-The_Lingo-New_York_City_New_York.html.

Meechan, Marjory Ellen. "The Mormon Drawl: Religious Ethnicity and Phonological Variation in Southern Alberta." PhD diss., University of Ottawa, 1999.

Memmott, Roger Ladd. *Heaven's Way*. N.p.: Gemstone Books, 2020.

Merriam-Webster Dictionary. https://www.merriam-webster.com/dictionary.

Miller, Zöe. "22 Phrases Americans Say That Leave Foreigners Completely Stumped." *Insider*, January 7, 2019. https://www.insider.com/confusing-things-americans-say-2018-4.

Morkel, Wendy McCollum. "Tracing a Sound Pattern: Ay Monophthongization in Utah English." Master's thesis, Brigham Young University, 2003.

Murphy, Lynne. "Can I Help Who's Next?" *Separated by a Common Language*. October 19, 2007. https://separatedbyacommonlanguage.blogspot.com/2007/10/can-i-help-whos-next.html.

Oger, Kimberly. "A Study of Non-Finite Forms of Anaphoric Do in the Spoken BNC." *Anglophonia, French Journal of English Linguistics* 28 (2019). https://journals.openedition.org/anglophonia/2936.

Online Slang Dictionary. http://onlineslangdictionary.com.

Oxford English Dictionary. https://www.oed.com.

Oxford Learner's Dictionaries. https://www.oxfordlearnersdictionaries.com/us.

Pardoe, T. Earle. "Some Studies of Rocky Mountain Dialects." *Quarterly Journal of Speech* 21, no. 3 (1935): 348–55.

Peterson, Michèle. "Phonetic Variation and Change: An Analysis of Steel and Still." *Deseret Language and Linguistic Society Symposium* 14 (1988): 47–55.

Phillips, J. *On the Drainage and Sewerage of Towns*. London: E & FN Spon., 1872.

The Phrase Finder. https://www.phrases.org.uk.

Pullum, Geoffrey. "Can I Help Who's Next?" *Language Log*. Last modified December 4, 2005. http://itre.cis.upenn.edu/~myl/languagelog/archives/002690.html.

R Core Team. R: A Language and Environment for Statistical Computing. V. 3.6. Linux/Mac/Windows, 2020.

Reeves, Larkin Hopkins. "Patterns of Vowel Production in Speakers of American English from the State of Utah." Master's thesis, Brigham Young University, 2009.

"Regional Vocabulary and Expressions within Québec." *Quebec Culture Blog*. February 3, 2015. https://quebeccultureblog.com/2015/02/03/regional-vocabulary-and-expressions-within-quebec-introduction-169/.

"Report: Three Utah Areas Top Nation in Population Growth." *U.S. New and World Report*, March 26, 2020. https://www.usnews.com/news/best-states/utah/articles/2020-03-26/report-3-utah-areas-top-nation-in-population-growth.

Rice University Neologisms Database. https://neologisms.rice.edu/index.php?a=term&d=1&t=4311.

Rosen, Nicole, and Crystal Skriver. "Vowel Patterning of Mormons in Southern Alberta, Canada." *Language and Communication* 42 (2015): 104–15.

Saad, J. T. "Document Resume." 1972. https://files.eric.ed.gov/fulltext/ED069030.pdf.

Salvesen, Anis. "What 770,000 Tubes of Saliva Reveal About America." *Ancestry*, February 8, 2017. https://blogs.ancestry.com/cm/what-770000-tubes-of-saliva-reveal-about-america/.

Sarver, Daniel A. "The Transferability of Utah English Characteristics: Second Dialect (D2) Acquisition in Utah." Honors thesis, Brigham Young University, 2004.

Savage, David Matthew. "How We Feel about How We Talk: A Language Attitude Survey of Utah English." Master's thesis, Brigham Young University, 2014.

Seol, Hyunsoo. SnowCluster: Cluster Analysis. [jamovi module]. 2020. https://github.com/hyunsooseol/snowCluster.

Shakespeare, William. *Othello: The Moor of Venice*. Edited by Mark Mussari. New York: Marshall Cavendish Benchmark, 2010.

Sledd, J. 1987. "A Canterbury Tell." *American Speech* 62 (1987): 185–86.

Sorenson, Kathryn Richards. *Personal History of Kathryn Richards Sorensen, 1987*. https://www.familysearch.org/service/records/storage/das-mem/patron/v2/TH-904-79685-1035-66/dist.txt?ctx=ArtCtxPublic.

Stanley, Joseph A. "Are Beg and Bag-Raising Distinct? Regional Patterns in Prevelar Raising in North American English." Paper presented at the American Dialect Society, New York, 2019.

Stanley, Joseph A., and Margaret E. L. Renwick. "Phonetic Shift /ɔr/ Phonemic Change? American English Mergers over 40 Years." Poster presented at *Laboratory Phonology 15*, Ithaca, New York, 2016.

Stanley, Joseph A., and Kyle Vanderniet. "Consonantal Variation in Utah English: What El[t]se is Happening[k]?" Paper presented at the 4th Annual Linguistics Conference, University of Georgia, Athens, Georgia, 2019.

Stopera, Matt, and Brian Galindo. "Do You Say These Things Like a Normal Person?" *Buzz-feed*, January 18, 2017. https://www.buzzfeed.com/mjs538/why-are-they-called-tennis-shoes-if-youre-not-even-playing-t.

Sykes, Robert D. "A Sociophonetic Study of (aɪ) in Utah English." Master's thesis, University of Utah, 2010.

Thomas, Erik R. "An Acoustic Analysis of Vowel Variation in New World English." Durham, NC: Duke University Press, 2001.

Tripp, George. 1989. "Tooele—What Is the Name's Origin?" *Utah Historical Quarterly* 57 (1989): 273–76.

Trudgill, Peter, ed. *Language in the British Isles*. Cambridge: Cambridge University Press, 1984.

Twain, Mark. *Adventures of Huckleberry Finn*. San Jose, CA: New Millennium Library, 2001.

United States Geological Survey. s.v. "fork." https://www.usgs.gov/search?keywords=fork.

Urban Dictionary. https://www.urbandictionary.com/define.

Vaux, Bert. "Dialects of American English Survey." 2018. https://www.dialectsofenglish.com/.

Vaux, Bert, and Scott Golder. "The Harvard Dialect Survey." Cambridge, MA: Harvard University Linguistics Department, 2003. http://dialect.redlog.net/.

Vaux, Bert, and Marius L. Jøhndal. Cambridge Online Survey of World Englishes, 2009. http://survey.johndal.com/results/.

Wells, John C. *Accents of English*. Vol. 2: *The British Isles*. Cambridge: Cambridge University Press, 1982.

Wilkins, Afton Lovell (Pettegrew). *Warts and All: Family Memories*. N.p.: Xlibris, 2010.

Williams, Hank. "Why Don't You Love Me?" Side A. MGM Records, 1950.

Wishydig, "(Oh) for ___!" Last updated June 26, 2009. https://wishydig.blogspot.com/2009/06/oh-for.html.

Wistisen, Sharon. *A Funny Thing Happened on the Way to the Farm*. N.p.: Xlibris, 2010.

Wolfram, Walt, and Natalie Schilling-Estes. *American English*. Cambridge: Cambridge University Press, 1998.

"World Population Review." 2020. https://worldpopulationreview.com/us-counties/states/ut.

Worthen, S. *Oral History of Mildred Vercimak*. 1989. https://newspaperarchive.com/soda-springs-sun-sep-24-1953-p-2.

Wu, Tim. "What Ever Happened to Google Books?" *New Yorker*, September 11, 2015. https://www.newyorker.com/business/currency/what-ever-happened-to-google-books.

Index

CPSIA information can be obtained
at www.ICGtesting.com
Printed in the USA
LVHW040036260623
750653LV00006B/87